HISTORICAL ARCHAEOLOGY
AND THE
IMPORTANCE OF MATERIAL THINGS

PAPERS OF THE THEMATIC SYMPOSIUM,
EIGHTH ANNUAL MEETING OF
THE SOCIETY FOR HISTORICAL ARCHAEOLOGY
CHARLESTON, SOUTH CAROLINA, JANUARY 7-11, 1975

LELAND FERGUSON
EDITOR

SPECIAL PUBLICATION SERIES, NUMBER 2
PUBLISHED AND REPRINTED BY
THE SOCIETY FOR HISTORICAL ARCHAEOLOGY
JOHN D. COMBES, EDITOR, 1977
J.W. JOSEPH, JOURNAL EDITOR, 2012

J.W. Joseph, SHA Journal Editor

Leland Ferguson
Editor

Reprinted, 2012
by the Society for Historical Archaeology
9707 Key West Avenue, Suite 100
Rockville, MD 20850

Published in the United States of America

Special Publication Series, Number 2
Published by

The Society for
Historical Archaeology

The painting on the cover of this volume
is by Darby Erd and was adapted from the
cover of the 1897 Sears Roebuck Catalogue,
published by Chelsea House Publishers, New
York, New York, 1968.

CONTENTS

Foreword to the 2012 Edition of *Historical Archaeology
and the Importance of Material Things* – J. W. Joseph i

Foreword – Stanley South 1

Preface – Leland Ferguson 3

Historical Archaeology and the Importance of Material Things – Leland Ferguson 5

Material Culture and Archaeology–What's the Difference? – James Deetz 9

Historical Archaeology–Is It Historical or Archaeological? – Lewis R. Binford 13

Archaeology and Folklore: Common Anxieties, Common Hopes – Henry Glassie 23

In Praise of Archaeology: Le Projet du Garbage – William L. Rathje 36

The New Mormon Temple in Washington, D.C. – Mark P. Leone 43

The Structure of Historical Archaeology and the
Importance of Material Things – James E. Fitting. 62

Afterword: "To Make Us Good People," A Reflection on the 1975
Thematic Symposium of the Annual Meeting of the Society for
Historical Archaeology, Charleston, South Carolina – Leland Ferguson 69

Foreword to the 2012 Edition of *Historical Archaeology and the Importance of Material Things*

In 1975 the Society for Historical Archaeology (SHA) convened its eighth annual meeting in Charleston, South Carolina under the direction of Conference Chair Stanley A. South. At that time, the discipline was still finding its theoretical and epistemological legs and South sought to move the field away from particularism and toward processualism with a symposium focused on theory in historical archaeology. He directed Leland Ferguson, his colleague at the University of South Carolina (USC), to organize such a session. With funding to support participant's travel, Ferguson developed a slate of figures that he felt could speak to historical archaeology's role in deciphering the past from different theoretical, geographic, and chronological perspectives.

Two of his proposed panelists, Robert Ascher and David Clarke, were unable to attend, but Ferguson was left with an impressive slate of archaeologists that included himself as well as Lewis Binford, Jim Deetz, Mark Leone, and Bill Rathje, and also folklorist Henry Glassie and archaeologist discussant James Fitting. The session was well received and the participants agreed to the publication of their papers, which appeared in 1977 as *Historical Archaeology and the Importance of Material Things,* edited by Leland G. Ferguson, the SHA's Second Special Publication (Ferguson 1977).

Importance would go on to multiple re-publications, including a final version that shed the by then battered original cover art by USC's

Darby Erd in favor of SHA journal's brown wrapper. SHA Editor Emeritus Ronn Michael tells me that this publication was easily the society's best-seller, and despite the fact that it has not seen print for more than 30 years, it is still used in coursework on development of the field. At the 2010 SHA Annual Meeting on Amelia Island I heard references to *Importance* in papers in multiple sessions and spoke with Leland Ferguson about the prospect of re-publishing the volume through the SHA's Print On Demand (POD) Press. Ferguson was enthusiastic, and also suggested that it might be time to consider an update. I then spoke to Julie Schablitsky, Chair of the SHA Baltimore 2012 Annual Meeting, about this prospect, and with that impetus, Schablitsky and co-editor Mark Leone have compiled a set of papers, *Historical Archaeology and the Importance of Material Things II,* that is also published through the SHA POD (Schablitsky and Leone 2012).

This republication of *Historical Archaeology and the Importance of Material Things* includes the original volume's contents: a Foreword by Stanley South and articles by Ferguson, Deetz, Binford, Glassie, Rathje, Leone, and Fitting, in that order. These are followed by an Afterword prepared by Leland Ferguson for this republication. I am pleased to see *Importance* back in print, as well as the discussion that should be generated as we look at historical archaeology of the last century and contrast it with our field in the new century, as presented in *Importance II* (Schablitsky and Leone 2012).

J. W. Joseph
Editor, *Historical Archaeology*

Bibliography

FERGUSON, LELAND (ED.)
    1977   *Historical Archaeology and the Importance of Material Things.* Special Publication Series, No. 2. The Society for Historical Archaeology. Columbia, South Carolina.

SCHABLITSKY, JULIE M. AND MARK P. LEONE (EDS.)
    2012   *Historical Archaeology and the Importance of Material Things II.* Special Publication Series, No 9. The Society for Historical Archaeology, Rockville, Maryland.

Foreword

When Robert L. Stephenson, host and general chairman for the eighth annual meeting of the Society for Historical Archaeology, asked that I act as program chairman for the Charleston event, I welcomed the opportunity. He knew of my concern and disappointment in the fact that the seven previous meetings of the Society for Historical Archaeology had focused on historical-descriptive, particularistic topics, with little concern shown for the idea-sets under which such topics were explored. I saw this as an opportunity likely to arise but once in a decade, to structure an SHA program around the belief system under which archaeology is undertaken, rather than around the data base addressed by that faith.

I envisioned a thematic framework emphasizing theory on the first day, method on the second day, and the usual descriptive papers on the final day of the conference. However, Leland Ferguson, whom I had asked to chair the thematic presentation, had a far better idea, pointing out that a session hailed as exploring theoretical concepts would likely be attended by very few, whereas one dealing with the importance of material things would attract a far wider audience. To insure as wide an audience as possible, including those who normally might be reluctant to attend a nondescriptive session, the thematic session was not concurrent with another session. Our concern over a lack of support for such an idea session was at that point a reflection of our awareness of the developmental background of historical archaeology, and our recognition that the field was not traditionally oriented to the testing of ideas. We had not yet discussed the session in terms of the participants, and as it turned out, those who agreed to join Leland in an examination of the importance of material things brought to the session credentials enough to insure a full auditorium under any conditions. Our fears regarding the reception of such a session are recorded here as a matter of historical record monitoring attitudes present in January 1975.

The strategy we had was that if we could bring together in one room an idea-set composed of Leland G. Ferguson, David L. Clarke, Lewis R. Binford, Henry Glassie, James Deetz, William Rathje, Mark Leone, and James Fitting, each bringing his own vibrant concepts, that something might happen similar to when drops of mercury are brought close together; a sudden coalescence might occur to produce a result larger than any of the parts. Those who attended the Charleston meeting are well aware that such a happening did occur.

As the reader enjoys the enclosed papers of Ferguson and his colleagues, an awareness of the importance of the Charleston meeting will begin to emerge in the image of the future of historical archaeology that these papers mirror.

The rare happening recognized here in this special volume by the Board of Directors of the Society for Historical Archaeology and its editor, John D. Combes, is seen as a pivotal event in historical archaeology. The Society for Historical Archaeology is indebted to special volume editor, Leland G. Ferguson, and production editor, Susan Jackson, for seeing this work to press.

It is difficult to say when another such event as the Charleston meeting will come about, given the depth to which particularism is endemic in historical archaeology. However, a revolution in thought is underway in the field, and its seeds are clearly seen in these papers. From such conceptual roots a new vitality will evolve in the decades to come through the process of exploring and testing our ideas about the past.

Stanley South
Institute of Archeology
and Anthropology
University of South Carolina

Preface

In the spring of 1974 when Stanley South, program chairman for the 1975 meeting of the Society for Historical Archaeology, asked me to develop a thematic symposium on theory for the meeting we were both excited. Our excitement stemmed from the opportunity of planning a general session for such a large group of archaeologists who dealt with historic sites. However, my excitement was somewhat curbed by apprehension. Sessions on "theory" were often stilted and polemic. They often proved divisive. The ideal, I thought, was a session that drew the variety of interests in the Society into an atmosphere of constructive interaction. The solution? We decided to have a symposium that would stress the most common interest of all archaeologists—material things. We would invite people, who regardless of their philosophy were convinced that there was a special value to be gained by studying the things people create. With this approach we felt that the variety of people attending the meetings would feel an affinity to the thematic symposium. There would be room for those of us religiously involved with science, for those who were historical particularists, for the humanist in us all and for the structuralists. The structuralists?

When this symposium was conceived there were no archaeologists that I knew of who were seriously involved with structuralism as an analytical approach to archaeology. True, James Deetz had alluded to a kind of structural approach in his introductory book, *Invitation to Archaeology*. Yet, no archaeologists had ever used and published a structural analysis. Nevertheless, when the symposium occurred and we all reflected on what had happened, we realized that three of the six invited participants explicitly acknowledged the value of a structural approach to archaeological materials. Indeed, Mark Leone's paper was a seminal structural analysis of a significant piece of American architecture. Subsequent to the symposium, Henry Glassie has published a structural analysis of eighteenth century houses in Virginia.

I shall not try to analyze this situation. Suffice it to say that I was as surprised as anyone else. I shall shed any claim to credit and shall insist on sharing any blame with fate for this interesting turn of circumstances. As James Fitting says in the last essay in this volume, "a symposium is a happening"—after a point it creates itself. The contents of this collection of essays are thus the written record of a happening, and I hope that as a collection it will be of value to archaeology.

The papers by Binford, Deetz, Rathje and myself are with only minor alterations as they were presented at the symposium. The contributions by Glassie and Leone have been reworked; however the revised versions serve only to clarify the presentations given in Charleston. James Fitting's comments at the symposium as well as those in this volume were both practical and cogent, and I sincerely thank him for accepting and completing this difficult task.

In concluding these prefatory remarks I would like to thank several people. Stanley South's inspiration and encouragement are directly responsible for the existence of this volume. He and John Combes were instrumental in securing the necessary funds from the state of South Carolina for the transportation of some of the participants. Robert L. Stephenson, Director of the Institute of Archeology and Anthropology, allowed us the time and opportunity to develop this symposium. To all of the participants in the symposium I extend my thanks for their generous contributions. Although they were not able to participate, I would also like to thank Robert Ascher and David Clarke for their ideas, their interest and their encouragement. The drawings accompanying the various essays as well as the art work for the cover were done by Darby Erd, and I am most appreciative for his interest and his contribution. Finally, I would like to thank Dick Carrillo, Annette Ferguson, Susan Jackson, J. Jefferson Reid, and Carol Speight for their helpful suggestions concerning the basic plans for this symposium.

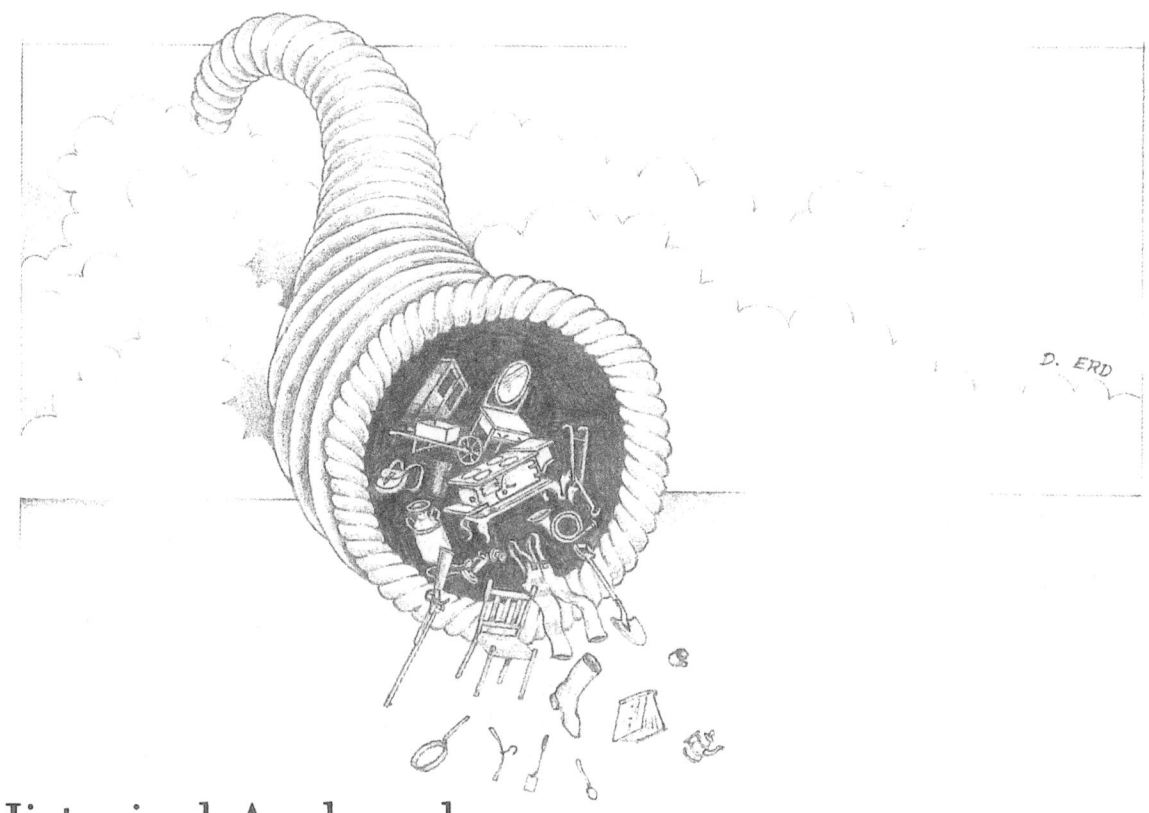

D. ERD

Historical Archaeology and the Importance of Material Things

Leland Ferguson

EARLY IN 1974 Stanley South asked me to chair a symposium on archaeological theory that would serve as a thematic session for these meetings. My response was to be honored, to be insecure, and to be frightened at the task of selecting a topic and speakers appealing to the variety of scholars attending these meetings.

This problem seemed best resolved by reducing our interests to their lowest common denominator. I believe our most common ground is the data we observe; and I believe that our most common desire is to develop meaningful interpretations about our fellow human beings and ourselves from those data. As a result, this symposium will concentrate on the importance of archaeological data—material things—and the undeveloped potential of those data.

The selection of panelists for this session was much simpler than the selection of the topic. I simply wrote down the names of the people I would most like to hear speak on the subject. To my amazement and sincere pleasure, most of those people are here with us today. The two notable exceptions are Robert Ascher and David Clarke. Dr. Ascher was interested in the symposium; however a sabbatical leave to study in South America as well as other interests prevented his being with us. Until about three weeks ago, Dr. Clarke was planning to be with us. However, his mother has been stricken with a serious illness, and this has prevented his leaving England at this time. He has asked me to extend his apologies to the Society, and to note that only a serious problem such as this could have prevented his being with us. On behalf of the Society I expressed our sorrow at the unfortunate circumstances of his absence.

As an introduction, I would like to review

some recent events that may have bearing on the papers of the symposium. In 1967, there was a heated debate concerning the activities of historical archaeologists. Pivoting around a paper by Clyde Dollar concerning "Some Thoughts on Theory and Method in Historical Archaeology," *The Conference on Historic Site Archaeology Papers* (1968) included forum comments from many authors concerning the goals of historical archaeology. While most of the discussion in this forum centered around theoretical positions and the problems of incompetence, there was an emphasis placed upon material culture as being an important body of data for use in the understanding of behavior. Stanley South (1968) in his forum response stated, "As archaeologists, it seems to me that we are concerned with the identification and interpretation of data reflecting patterned human behavior." In his emphasis on pattern, South was reflecting on the kinds of regularities recognized by Harrington (1954) for pipestems, Dethlefsen and Deetz (1966) for the decorative elements on New England grave stones, Glassie (1971) for traditional American artifacts, Leone (1973) for Mormon fences, and South (1972) himself for English colonial ceramics. The success of these scholars in isolating regularities within the material remains of historical American culture continually reinforces our awareness that perhaps as important as the ideas people happen to write down are the things they leave behind.

Unfortunately, the "things people leave behind" have seldom received the attention they deserve. Yet, the lack of attention has not been because we didn't care. The neglect seems to have developed as a result of our archaeology being so firmly fostered in its youth by ethnology and history. These fields have not traditionally emphasized material things; rather, they have concentrated on the abstract aspects of the social, economic, political, and ideological subsystems of culture. Moreover, their data are derived from direct communication or observation of the people being studied. The pattern, and most importantly the potential, of the material things that people have left behind has usually gone unnoticed by both the people and the social scientists.

Important things have happened within the past ten to fifteen years that seem to be changing the direction and emphasis of archaeology. Archaeologists have begun to recognize the uniqueness of their data, and the existence of conceptual models that fit these data and help to explain the behavior that produced it.

Transition from the traditional ethnological alignment of archaeology to a recognition of the importance of archaeological data may be seen in the changing attitudes of specific archaeologists. James Deetz, a pioneer in the attempt to examine the dynamics of ethnographically defined social change through the use of archaeological data, warned in 1968 that the use of such studies should always be considered in the light of their potential contribution to the broader understanding of culture, or take their place as mere exercises in "methodological virtuosity." Deetz' point was that simply showing you can archaeologically come up with information that corresponds to an ethnographical classification does not necessarily contribute to the understanding of culture. (However, it does demonstrate the power of archaeological techniques.) Speaking more directly to this point, Deetz stated (1970:122),

> . . . I'm struck by the fact that there seems to be some sort of feeling on the part of archaeologists that the categories used by the ethnographer are possessed of somewhat greater cultural truth than the categories which he imposes on his own data. There is a genuine problem here. It seems that to seek a one-to-one relationship between two different products of similar behavior runs a considerable risk of distortion. It is rather like addition of apples and pears. The categories which have been devised by ethnologists to describe the cultural universe they study need not be, and in fact should not be, the categories which the archaeologists seek correspondence in their data.

Reinforcing this statement by Deetz, Marvin Harris (1968), an ethnologist, admonished archaeologists to rid themselves of the attempt to force their data into the categories defined by ethnographers. Harris held that archaeologists had developed efficient, objective tools for the understanding of behavior, and that perhaps ethnologists should look to find equivalents of the archaeological categories in their own subjectively contaminated data.

Perhaps the most concise and apt statement

of this idea about archaeology has been presented by British archaeologist David Clarke (1968:13) when he says,

> . . . archaeology, is archaeology, is archaeology (with apologies to Gertrude Stein). Archaeology is a discipline in its own right, concerned with archaeological data which it clusters in archaeological entities displaying certain archaeological processes and studied in terms of archaeological aims, concepts, and procedures.

> An archaeological culture is not a racial group, nor a historical tribe, nor a linguistic unit, it is simply an archaeological culture.

At no point does Clarke deny the relationship between an archaelogical complex and the other aspects of culture. However, he does treat the relationship between concepts founded on different data as a special topic for consideration. In his treatment of *Analytical Archaeology* (1968), he first examines the world of past material culture. Then he considers the relationship between this material model of the past and the established cultural processes that may have been responsible for the archaeological patterns. He is quick to point out that relating one kind of data to the processes established on the basis of another requires sophisticated transformations.

Although these statements by Deetz, Harris, and Clarke are primarily from the world of anthropological archaeology, this fledgling dictum also holds for the relationship between history and archaeology. Rephrasing Deetz' comments, we may say that the historical document does not necessarily contain more truth than the artifacts recovered from the ground. Nor, is the structure of phenomena as interpreted through history necessarily more valid than the structure observed and interpreted by the archaeologist. The historical and the archaeological records are different analogs of human behavior, and they should not necessarily be expected to coincide.

Perhaps as important as the recognition of the uniqueness of archaeological data has been the concomitant development of an attitude about the theoretical context of archaeological research. During the early part of the last decade, Lewis Binford (1962), amid a sea of controversy, implored archaeologists to adopt a sound, theoretically founded, approach to their studies. Binford proposed that the cultural theory posited by Leslie White, considering culture as means of adaptation with technology as a primary adaptive operative, was especially suited for use with archaeological data. Of course, other archaeologists have proposed other approaches to the understanding of the data. The important point is that the pressure of Binford and others has forced archaeologists to become introspective and to consider the ultimate value of their research. The resulting effect has been a trend for archaeologists to investigate well defined problems that are congruent with archaeological data. To me, one of the most exciting things about modern archaeology must be that this trend is only the beginning.

Drawing together these ideas and, I hope, the general intent of these archaeologists, I feel that we are beginning to see a strong convergence of attitude in archaeology, settling on the point that there is far more value in archaeological data than most of us have previously recognized. With carefully considered theoretical positions and a rigorous treatment of the data, archaeology (including prehistoric, historic, and modern archaeology) can be one of the most powerful tools available for understanding human behavior. Archaeology need not, and should not be the handmaiden of ethnology, history or any other field of study. Controlling a special expression of human behavior, archaeology can go about the business of treating the problems that may be clarified by an examination of the material evidence of culture. That is, if archaeology is to fulfil itself, it must expand beyond the conceptual world of disciplines that do not handle the data available to archaeologists.

There is so much data available to historical archaeologists that it staggers the imagination. The historical period in North America from the seventeenth century through the present day has been marked by an ever increasing proliferation of material items. Farm tools, ceramics, houses, furniture, toys, buttons, roads, cities, villages—the list continues almost *ad infinitum* and includes all of the things people make from the physical world.

Most of us here today are archaeologists, and

we are planning to do something with this kind of data. We can look at it, describe it, draw it, photograph it, count it, and write about it. However, if we think as historians and ethnologists we shall provide no more than incidental information to history and ethnology. The process is somewhat akin to trying to play golf with a tennis racquet. The problem is that once we recognize our situation we have to go about finding a golf club. The members of this symposium entertain somewhat different theoretical positions. Yet, it is clear from their writings that they have all developed a firm conviction that material data have a potential to contribute fundamentally to the understanding of human behavior. I feel that the discipline of historical archaeology will benefit significantly if this symposium stimulates us to more fully recognize and respect the potential power of the data we control. Such recognition may encourage us to develop new and imaginative ways of fulfilling our intellectual goals through analysis of the "things people leave behind."

Institute of Archeology and Anthropology
University of South Carolina

Bibliography

BINFORD, LEWIS R.
1962 Archaeology as anthropology. *American Antiquity* 28 (2): 217–225.

CLARKE, DAVID
1968 *Analytical archaeology*. Methuen & Co., Ltd., London.

DEETZ, JAMES F.
1968 The inference of residence and descent rules from archaeological data. In *New perspectives in archeology*, edited by Sally R. Binford and Lewis R. Binford, pp. 41–48. Aldine Atherton, Chicago.
1970 Archeology as a social science. In Current directions in anthropology, *Bulletin of the American Anthropological Association* 3 (3), part 2: 115–125.

DETHLEFSEN, E. and J. DEETZ
1966 Death's heads, cherubs, and willow trees: experimental archaeology in colonial cemeteries. *American Antiquity* 31 (4): 502–510.

DOLLAR, CLYDE
1968 Some thoughts on theory and method in historical archaeology. *The Conference on Historic Site Archaeology Papers 1967* 2, part 2: 3–30.

GLASSIE, HENRY
1971 *Pattern in the material folk culture of the eastern United States*. University of Pennsylvania Press, Philadelphia.

HARRINGTON, J. C.
1954 Dating stem fragments of seventeenth and eighteenth century clay tobacco pipes. *Archaeological Society of Virginia, Quarterly Bulletin* 9 (1): 6–8.

HARRIS, MARVIN
1968 Comments. In *New perspectives in archeology*, edited by Sally R. Binford and Lewis R. Binford, pp. 359–361. Aldine Atherton, Chicago.

LEONE, MARK
1973 Archaeology as the science of technology: Mormon town plans and fences. In *Research and theory in current archaeology*, edited by Charles L. Redman, pp. 125–150. Wiley-Interscience, New York.

SOUTH, STANLEY
1968 Comments on 'Some thoughts on theory and method in historical archaeology' by Clyde Dollar. *The Conference on Historic Site Archaeology Papers 1967* 2, part 2: 35–53.
1972 Evolution and horizon as revealed in ceramic analysis in historical archaeology. *The Conference on Historic Site Archaeology Papers 1971* 6: 71–116.

Material Culture and Archaeology— What's the Difference?

James Deetz

I'D LIKE TO PREFACE THIS PAPER with the sincere request that it not be taken too seriously. One of the lessons that I think I'm learning as I advance into the sunset toward senior citizenship is that the most important thing in life is not to take it deadly serious, because all you do is get yourself into trouble. Still, in all, I think that buried within the morass of things I have to say are a couple of points that might at least bear thinking about, and maybe they deserve a bit of extended consideration.

About the title—I think I have an international reputation as the worst title writer in the world. I simply cannot produce them. Anyone who calls something "The Doppler Effect in Archaeological Chronology: In Consideration of the Spatial Aspects of Seriation," (Deetz and Dethlefsen 1965) complete with colon, should

be shot. But, I figure starting from there, there's nowhere to go but up, so Leland and I kind of put the title of this paper together. The first half of this title is a statement of subject; the second half asks a question. Obviously, there are a number of answers to this question, which we have all considered. Yet it is possible that we have not completely appreciated the range and diversity and the concomitant importance of material culture to the study of human behavior, now and in the past.

A cursory review of traditional definitions and concepts tells us that material culture and artifacts are vaguely synonymous. "They are the products of man's technology," or "all those things made by man," or "they are referred to as cultural material rather than material culture." Of course all these considerations have their value, but we must look for the definition or definitions that will have the most value to archaeologists.

As archaeologists we must deal with artifacts and consider their subterranean context. From this perspective material culture is culturally patterned data which provide the archaeologist with insights to life in the past. Viewed in this fashion, the difference between archaeology and material culture is one of scope. Archaeology is the discipline or subdiscipline, and material culture —that is artifacts—is the set of most culturally sensitive data available. Such a view of the relationship between material culture and archaeology is from within, so to speak; and certainly all historical archaeologists and most probably most, if not all, prehistorians have a more catholic view of material culture than that above. However, among the other precincts of anthropology, material culture is not ranked as important to the student of the human species, simply because the folks are there too, and one can go directly to the behavior being studied without going through the screen produced by the material culture in between.

Certainly the questions asked of material culture by most ethnographers and ethnologists are of a very different order and emphasis than that asked by archaeologists. "Pots and pans" courses are considered relatively unimportant in most universities. The real "substance" of anthropology is more likely to be sought in courses in structural anthropology or kinship algebra. Perhaps to anthropologists, material culture has been as the elephant to the blind man. Each encounters a different part and reacts differently in accordance with the precise circumstances of the contact.

Possibly a modest and tentative redefinition of material culture is in order. Perhaps through redefinition the elephant can better be perceived for what it truly is. Consider material culture as that segment of man's physical environment which is purposely shaped by him according to culturally dictated plans. This definition will more than comfortably accommodate all which we have considered as material culture thus far: Siberian fish hooks, office buildings, banjos, Freaky cereal and the little band of

plastic Freakies which dwells in the box, the box, standing rib roast, apple pies, jumbo jets, step ladders, Venus figurines, and a number of other objects too numerous to mention here. But what of topiary work or perennial borders of flowers? This query is not quite as silly as it might seem at first. These things differ from those mentioned above in that they are living. Nevertheless, when we cut a privet, or shape a dwarf pine tree, we are modifying real world material according to a set of cultural plans.

Now, with animate beings the problem of endowing them with a culturally dictated form is a bit more complex. Yet, this is not to say that there are not a great number of ways whereby man also shapes the animate sector of his environment, including himself, in culturally ordained ways. The end result of this kind of modification is just as much material culture as is our beloved shell edged pearlware or a Pomo basket. Of course, a number of examples may come to mind of material culture formed by alteration of the human physique. Such things as scarification and tatooing are worked on living people, but much of the design could equally be applied to paper or wood. Of a very different order is the way man uses his physique alone or in the company of others to accomplish various tasks and follow the set of culturally prescribed rules in doing so. This range of cultural phenomena has been extensively studied, but not studied as material culture. Kinesics is concerned with the obviously cultural manipulation of the individual by himself, but it seems inescapable to view this too as material culture. Perhaps less obvious is the range of behavior which is covered by the study of proxemics; yet here too is a case of arranging a sector of the environment, in this instance people, according to a set of cultural rules.

At this point, one might object that there is a significant difference between a person kneeling in prayer, material culture by the definition above, and a harpoon. After all, once the prayer is ended the individual assumes another form; but the harpoon will remain a harpoon indefinitely, perhaps for millenia. Yet the ephemeral nature of the phenomena seems spurious criteria for definition. A simple illustration of this is a piece of rope being used by a Boy Scout in passing his tenderfoot knot-tying test. The same rope can be folded into sheep shank, half hitch, and bowline. Each is a piece of material culture enduring perhaps only for seconds.

I have suggested elsewhere (Deetz 1967) that technologies may be divided into additive and subtractive categories. Additive technologies involve the aggregation of raw materials, such as quilling a basket, and are in theory at least, infinitely expandable. Subtractive technologies are those which involve material removal such as carving or stone work, and artifact size is a function of the size of the parent block of stone, wood, bone, or other substance. To these, we might add another category, manipulative, in which neither adding nor removing of materials is involved, but only the reshaping of the constant mass. Examples of manipulative artifacts include blown glass, oragami, the knots mentioned above, as well as the endless variety of ways in which man uses his body to communicate, to work, and to play.

The proxemic use of the human body as a unit of material culture may go beyond simple considerations of what is usually called cultural space, to the entire range of ways in which man, in numbers, creates culturally patterned phenomena. In this case, the people may become involved as components of a set of larger systems, and the individuals perform much the same function as individual, unmodified grass stems in the foundation of a coiled basket. Highly structured examples of this class of material culture are parades or rituals involving large numbers of individuals. The Catholic High Mass before Vatican II is a striking instance involving kinesic, proxemic, and even larger scale patterns. The complex and often bizarre configurations performed on football fields during halftime such as a band forming the word "OHIO" is, as far as I'm concerned, just as much material culture as an arrowhead.

Less structured and correspondingly less obvious examples of this phenomenon include communities and families. If we can accept the culturally patterned assemblage of family members within a household as material culture under the definition offered above, then it becomes obvious that a whole range of data normally in the domain of the ethnologist

should also be considered from the material perspective. The same applies to the disposition of these family units into aggregates called communities. One definition of an archaeological assemblage is simply the material remains of a community. However, we must remember that communities are composed of people. In reality, the community and the archaeological assemblage are one. The living component of the assemblages, subassemblages, and artifacts identified in archaeology may only be ignored at our peril.

A shovel does not excavate by itself, but is attached to a shoveler who shovels in a manner dictated by his culture. His motor habits are learned and culturally determined, and it is probably fair to say that both shovel form and shoveler form must be understood. For instance, seventeenth century shovels cannot be used with the same motor habits we use with modern shovels. Likewise, dwelling houses are used by dwellers, and while the form of the house is dictated by the number of and relationship between the dwellers it must, in turn, also impose a structure upon them. The relationship between the human and inanimate components of these systems is not a one way street. Behavior is reflected in material culture to be sure, but material culture, especially as it is considered here, is reflected in behavior as well.

In the realm of language, I have suggested elsewhere (Deetz 1967) that material culture in the traditional sense and language are homologous, as well as analogous to each other. If this is so then it is no surprise that all the structural and syntactic analyses of language have such ready application to artifacts. The homology is derived simply from the fact that the physical form of language is that of a modified substance. The substance is air and the modification is in the size and shape of the vibrating air mass and the frequency variations imparted to it by the vocal cords. This class of culturally shaped substance can neither be seen nor touched, but it is as much a part of man's culturally modified physical environment as is a brick schoolhouse. I suspect that if linguists had been able to stack their words on tables like potsherds, the insights they have developed concerning the structure and syntax of language may well have been much slower in developing. Whether such is the case or not, the linguists were the first to demonstrate the precise structural form of a patterned cultural phenomenon, and even though the terms "formeme" and "facteme" are rather atrocious in their etymological bastardization, this does not detract from what I believe to be their reality in an homologous as well as analogous sense. Likewise, efforts to apply the techniques of linguistics to more .complex material configurations, when they have succeeded, owe part of their success to the same homology. It has been suggested that people and their language can be accommodated under a somewhat revised and more general definition of material culture.

There is always the danger in broadening definitions to such a point that they lose their precision. Years ago, I made up a semi-facetious definition of culture that I actually thought was rather good, only to have a student point out that it also defined a spiral nebula, God, and an ant hill. In this case, however, such a generalization is not indicated, and yet, many other cultural phenomena not normally thought of as material culture do fall promptly within the bounds of this definition. Consider, for example, animal domestication. To the extent that the form of these animals has been dictated by cultural preference, we can see domestication as a process of material culture production. This may not apply too directly to animals such as the dogs that lived among North American Indians, but in the case of a color coordinated living room complete with white cat and black dog, the process seems disturbingly complete. Also, as we learn more of the complexity of human genetics and its code, we can expect a time to come when purposeful alteration of the human body will be effected. When this happens yet another dimension of the use of the body as an artifact will have emerged.

As we consider the way in which a simple change in the definition of material culture broadens its applicability, it becomes increasingly clear that as archaeologists we have been laboring under a needless burden for these many years. All of those behavioral scientists have really been poaching on our domain, but we haven't reacted since we didn't know where the property line was. One thing about these poachers—they use some very effective weapons. So, whether we decide to evict them or not, their arms should be incorporated into our analytical arsenal. Claude Lévi-Strauss has a delightful way of turning things upside down for a better look at them, as indicated in one of my favorite passages from his writing, *Tristes Tropiques* (1970), second chapter, and I quote, "The fact that my first glimpse of British University life was in the neo-Gothic precincts of the University of Daka in eastern Bengal, has since made me regard Oxford as part of India that has got its mud, humidity, and super abundant vegetation under surprisingly good control." Perhaps in a similar manner we have inverted the relationships between material culture, archaeology, and the rest of anthropology. The time may have arrived to inform our fellow anthropologists that the poor cousin, material culture, has at last come into its true place in the order of things. This new order would hold the study of material culture to be the proper study of man. Its subdisciplines would include ethnography, ethnology, and archaeology. Anthropology departments would be material culture departments, and as we expand and define our jargon, we may soon be asking, "Is the study of material culture a science?"

Department of Anthropology
Brown University

Bibliography

DEETZ, JAMES
    1967 *Invitation to archaeology.* American Museum Science Books, New York.
DEETZ, JAMES and EDWIN DETHLEFSEN
    1965 The Doppler effect and archaeology: a consideration of the spatial aspects of seriation. *Southwestern Journal of Anthropology* 21 (3): 196–206.
LÉVI-STRAUSS, CLAUDE
    1970 *Tristes tropiques.* Atheneum, New York.

D. ERD

Historical Archaeology
Is It Historical
or Archaeological?

Lewis R. Binford

IT'S NEW YEARS DAY 1975. I am trying to prepare a paper for presentation at a conference on historical archaeology. Do I have anything to say?

This was the setting and my thoughts as I began preparation of this paper. Then I began to think along the following lines. If this was a conference on archaeology I would have no problem. I have unpublished material relevant to many subjects of general archaeological interest. Obviously my problem arose from the "historical" orientation of the conference. Why? Why should I be uncomfortable and indecisive as to an appropriate subject or way of treating a problem. I continued to be uneasy with "historical." Clearly I felt that persons doing "historical" archaeology were different from myself with different interests. Why? Cer-

tainly it is not because of specially relevant or technical information which is part of the "information pool" of persons working in sites of relatively recent age in North America. I can talk creamware and kaolin pipes with the best of them. Why? That word "historical" again! What does it mean? Well, it means that there is information available from the past in addition to the archaeological record. It means that the past may be investigated with resources other than those provided solely by archaeological investigation. Great—wonderful—that should mean historic archaeologists should be more sophisticated and better informed. Specialists in this field should provide the most informative tests or evaluations of ideas set forth by archaeologists in general. They should be in the forefront in theory building. Why in god's name

13

am I hesitant—I should be jumping up and down with anticipation. I was not. Back to that word "historical" again.

It must mean more than just having nonarchaeological information surviving from the past. Yes, sadly it does mean more—it implies a philosophy, an epistemology, and a value system in operation among the adherents. How does a Unitarian say anything of relevance to a congregation of fundamentalists, or a chiropractor excite the assembled American Medical Association? On the other hand, are my conceptions of historical archaeologists incorrect? This is a conference, and presumably its advantage stems from discussion and interaction ideally aimed at understanding. Okay, instead of delivering a paper on how to do science perhaps based on an incorrect appreciation of the audience, I have decided on another approach. I will relate some relatively recent experiences which I consider revealing and informative about the process of attempting to do archaeological science. Perhaps these experiences, when discussed, will promote a more constructive conference on how to advance archaeology regardless of the adjectives preceeding the word.

One hundred and thirty six Eskimos are settled in a permanent village at Anaktuvuk Pass, Alaska. One steps off the commercial plane which currently delivers mail twice a week and is immediately struck with a number of very deceiving features. Used oil drums, some rusting, others with the distinctive State of Alaska blue paint seem to dominate the land. A visitor remarked "I had the feeling I was entering a migrant workers' camp in central California." The people around the plane are dressed in a wide variety of clothes, some donated by missionaries, some abandoned by visitors, others freshly arrived from the mail-order houses of the "lower 48." The visitor arriving as I did in 1969 to learn about the Eskimos' ways of relating to their treeless tundra world seize upon certain features for reassurance. Some wear "traditional" parkas in spite of their being made of mail-order cloth. There were racks for drying and storing meat scattered throughout the village. Roughly fifty percent of the visible houses were "traditional." These were hard to see because of the new boxes made of plywood and

painted in a variety of blues and yellows which obscured the low lying houses built of earth and blending with the colors of the land. My disappointment must have shown. I had read of the Nunamiut, the Caribou hunters of the central Brooks range. I had carefully planned to live and work with these people in order to learn which strategies must be followed to cope successfully with their tundra world. Some ninety miles north of the arctic circle, two hundred miles from the nearest community, these facts seemed irrelevant. The modern world had engulfed the most remote part of the rugged sawtooth mountains in Alaska's arctic. I noted the younger teenagers wearing Beatle boots and the first undercut suggestions lead me to predict that when I came again the boys would be wearing long hair.

I walked up into the village with the children pulling at me asking, "What's your name?" Then coming down the path a man "late for the plane" said with a shy smile "my name is Johnny Rulland." He wore a dingy pair of Air Force dress blue pants, a torn and greasy "ski jacket," and a small baseball cap. This was the man I was to contact, the man whom I had arranged to work with for learning about hunting strategies! I offered a kind of forced smile, trying to hide from him and myself my disappointment. I know this world of "poverty," this world of donated clothes, and the absence of waste disposal collectors. I felt oddly at home when I had anticipated a world about which I knew nothing!

We pitched our tents on the east side of the airstrip and began to unpack. The children were all around, pulling on our arms, "come see the nest over here." "You want to fish?" "You got hooks?" "I'll catch fish for you." I looked at my watch, two thirty in the morning! My god, these kids should be in bed. I should be in bed! Yet the sun was still shining and one would judge from a New Mexico summer perspective that it was about eight o'clock in the evening. The environment hadn't changed. I tried to sleep with the light coming through the tent walls; instead I thought about why I had come and what I had hoped to accomplish.

I had become excited by the prospects of doing "living archaeology" with this group of people when Nicholas Gubser's book (1965) on his experiences here in 1962 was published. At that time I was deeply involved in research on the Mousterian materials from southern France. Some two years later I became convinced that if we were going to make sense out of the Mousterian and its remarkable forms of variability, we needed some reliable behavioral context in terms of which variability in stone tools could be studied. I had summarized this interest in a research proposal as follows:

A number of challenges have recently been offered to the views which have traditionally guided archaeological interpretation. For instance, Francois Bordes has convincingly demonstrated that lithic assemblages of the Middle Paleolithic, or Mousterian, do not exhibit regular directional trends through time (Bordes 1961), the pattern which archaeologists have come to expect as "normal." Rather, through a sequence of deposits from a single location, variations in the artifact composition from discrete occupational episodes often exhibit an alternating pattern so that tool frequencies from a level in the middle of the deposit might resemble most closely those from the bottom or top of the site, rather than resembling most closely the depositionally adjacent assemblages. In addition to demonstrating a lack of directional change, Bordes has also been able to show that there are four basic forms of Mousterian assemblage, as measured by the relative frequencies of tool types. Three major propositions were advanced to explain this well documented and apparently unpatterned alternation of types of Mousterian assemblage through sequences of occupations:

(1) The different types of Mousterian assemblage are the result of seasonal patterns of living, with each type representing different seasonal remains.

(2) Each kind of assemblage represents a slightly different adaptation to a different environment, the forms of the assemblage being directly determined by climatic alternations through time.

(3) Each type of assemblage represents the remains of different groups of people, each group characterized by its own distinctive complement of tools. The alternation of industries reflects the variations in the spatial distribution of these groups through time.

Bordes has been able to argue convincingly that the data do not support the first two arguments; he therefore tentatively accepted the third—that the four types of Mousterian assemblage were associated with different Neanderthal "tribes" (Bordes 1961). I have argued (Binford and Binford 1966) that some variability among assemblages is ignored in Bordes' classification of assemblage types and secondly that much of the interassemblage variability is to be understood as the by-product of different activities having been conducted at various locations in the context of an essentially nonsedentary hunting and gathering adaptation. I have further suggested that much of the variability can be understood as expected differences between base camps versus hunting and gathering stations, kill sites, and other functionally specific locations related to extractive versus maintenance tasks. Contrary to these views Bordes (1968: 144) argued, based largely on the thickness of some archaeological deposits and the consistency of assemblage form in many thick deposits, that the sites were relatively permanent and group sizes were large.

I reasoned that if activity variability and its logistics were the proper context for understanding interassemblage variability documented by Bordes, then this should certainly be manifest in the faunal materials preserved. Following this lead, funds were sought from the National Science Foundation in 1968 for a complete study of the fauna from the deeply stratified site of Combe Grenal. Funds were granted and Sally Binford and I spent eleven months studying the fauna, tools, and other related phenomena of the uniquely varying Mousterian assemblages excavated by Bordes. Preliminary analysis revealed a number of interesting patterns which can be briefly summarized as follows:

(A) The number of animals represented in any one occupation zone are relatively few. Based on this observation it is reasonable to suggest that the occupations at the site of Combe Grenal were of relatively short duration and, although variable, group sizes were generally small.

(B) There are clear differences observable be-

15

tween species and groups of animal species in the relative frequencies of anatomical parts represented.

(1) Bovids and horses: These animals are represented by analogous anatomical parts and are clearly differentiated from reindeer and deer in the parts present.

  (a) Bovids are primarily represented by mandibular fragments, lower teeth, fragments of the tibia, femur, humerus, and radio-cubitus. Ribs, vertebrae, pelvic parts, skull fragments, metapodials, and phalanges are rare.

  (b) Horses are primarily represented by mandibular fragments, lower teeth, fragments of tibia, femur, humerus, and radio-cubitus. In contrast to the bovids there is much greater variability in the frequency of maxillary teeth. In some levels maxillary teeth exceed counts of mandibular teeth. The latter generally occurs in levels with numerous horses represented. As in the case of bovids, ribs, vertebrae, pelvic parts, skull fragments, metapodials, and phalanges are rare.

(2) Deer and reindeer: There are greater differences between these two animals in the parts represented; nevertheless they bear more analogies to each other than either does to bovids and horses.

  (a) There is much greater variability between different occupations in the anatomical parts represented than is the case for either bovids or horses.

  (b) All previously described patterns of variation in anatomical parts are represented among the deer and reindeer remains from the occupations of Combe Grenal. Frequencies analogous to those noted on kill sites (White 1954; Kehoe 1967; Dibble and Lorrain 1968) are represented. Similarly, frequencies analogous to two recognized patterns documented for semipermanent settlements on the plains of North America (Wood 1962) are also represented. In addition there are patterns of variation not previously documented.

(C) There are marked and contrastive patterns of variability in the anatomical parts represented from a single species recovered from different occupational zones in Combe Grenal.

(D) There are no bone samples from Combe Grenal in which all the anatomical parts of any animal are represented in expected proportional frequencies based on their frequency in the skeleton of the animal.

(E) There are clear correlations crosscutting the recognized types of assemblage between some tool types and the pounds of meat represented by certain species. In addition there are correlations crosscutting the recognized types of assemblages between some tools and the total amount of meat represented regardless of species.

(F) There are correlations crosscutting recognized types of assemblages between some tool types and particular parts of certain species.

(G) There is no demonstrable directional change in the patterns of variation among anatomical parts from the bottom to the top of the deposit.

(H) There are some correlations between faunal components and the four types of Mousterian assemblages recognized by Bordes.

In spite of the demonstrable variety in patterning noted among anatomical parts, and correlations between tools and fauna or faunal elements, these remain facts in need of explanation as did the original observations on stone tool variability. It is clear that without an understanding of the causes of archaeological variation in faunal elements, I am unable to suggest the behavioral contexts in which stone tools were used when correlations are demonstrated between tools and fauna; in short, without an explanation facts remain facts. Regardless of the accuracy of Bordes' "historical" interpretation, here were facts not easily accommodated and clearly sources of potential information about the past. Could they be understood in processual terms?

My original thoughts had been that the Nunamiut were primarily dependent upon a single terrestrial mammal—caribou. They had been, until around 1950, a fully mobile hunting and gathering band. They lived in the broken mountainous tundra. The Neanderthals who had occupied the site of Combe Grenal for part of its occupational span had lived in a full tundra in a broken, low mountainous setting. They had been heavily dependent upon reindeer—the European form of the New World caribou. They were also most probably mobile hunters. The Nunamiut provided the closest analogue to the conditions envisioned for the Neanderthals of any known contemporary society. I wanted therefore to observe behavior under conditions as closely analogous to the Neanderthal situation as possible. Clearly, the old men who could remember that way of life were the ones for me to concentrate upon. I had to do classic "salvage ethnography." I had to collect as much "memory culture" as possible. Finally, I went to sleep.

The June sun on the tent woke me around eleven o'clock the next morning. I crawled out, went down to the stream for water while the students prepared breakfast. While eating, we talked of the "old men." I recalled a picture in Helge Ingsted's book *Nunamiut* (1954). It was a magnificent picture of a smiling Eskimo with the wind whipping the long guard hairs of the wolf ruff around the hood of his parka. The caption had read "The Eskimo Paniaq, a matchless hunter and splendid story-teller" (p. 17). Simon Paneack is a famous man, practically every anthropologist to live with or visit the Nunamiut has obtained a large share of their information from him. I wondered if he would remember the locations where he had lived year by year, the details of hunting, caching, food preparation, and processing which I wanted to know in order to "understand" the variability in anatomical parts anticipated on the sites where he had lived before he became sedentary.

Coming through the low willows toward our camp was a man of medium height, walking slowly as he swished a green willow stick to drive off the morning crop of mosquitoes. He wore a pair of very baggy "oxford grey" pants and a pair of black "street shoes" like one associates with formal social occasions. He spoke first, "Do you fellows plan to stay very long?" I remember thinking how "good" his English was. I explained that we were "anthropologists" and wanted to learn about how his people had lived "before they settled at Anaktuvuk village." He said, "I'm Simon Paneack, what's your name." I felt faintly embarrased, like one feels on meeting a famous man who has fallen, or become an alcoholic. Paneack pulled up an empty Blazo can and we talked for some time. He drew us maps of where he had lived on various occasions at Tulugak Lake some miles north. He said he had killed his first bird while camped there in 1906. He said his parents had seen their first flour, obtained in trade from the Kobuk, while they were camped on the Killik River in 1892.

All this was noted in my small brown surveyers' notebook.

I was unable to make an appointment with Paneack for further questions in the afternoon. I had noted from the plane that there were caribou bones scattered on the tundra all around the village. I would walk out and examine these and record the parts abandoned in the field by hunters. A good sample of data from "kill sites" would come in handy to give me some idea of the parts of the animals given preferential treatment.

Once out of the village the environment began to scream its presence to my senses. Looking north across the tundra there was no discernible evidence that man had ever been there. Lakes were discovered behind almost every knoll, the mountains were magnificent giants standing mute with snowcaps around their high shoulders and cloud shrouded heads. It was easy to imagine groups of Neanderthal men in such a setting; it was easier to see Paneack as a young man with his dogs moving amongst these valley pathways in search of game. It was exciting. The kill sites were very reassuring, the bones lying around were identical to those that I had spent hours counting while at the archaeology laboratory at Bordeaux, France. I began to take the recording of kills seriously and became fascinated by the obvious differences between one and another.

I returned late that night to the village encouraged and began to ask questions of the younger men whom I was meeting gradually. I had met Noah Ahgook. My notebook records the following: "Noah is the Postmaster—I asked him about the unbutchered cows that I had seen and he replied that they were left on the tundra because too many were killed." He didn't want to talk about hunting and just smiled when I asked why some animals were represented by only heads, others by heads and lower legs, and others by many different combinations of parts. He said, "Sometimes we do it one way, other times another way—if you want to know about 'old timers' you will have to ask the old men." I hadn't said anything to Noah about "old timers." He of course knew I was an anthropologist since the word on new arrivals to Anaktuvuk travels fast. As one of my younger

17

Eskimo friends later explained it, "we know what anthropologists want to know—they come here to talk to the old men about the ways of the 'old timers.'" I recalled a class I had had in "Ethnographic Field Methods" at the University of North Carolina. As a class project each student was to study a nearby local community. I had selected a Church congregation in the small community of Union Grove, North Carolina. I had been counseled to tell the people I was an historian "because if they hear you are an anthropologist they may shy away thinking you want to learn about their sex practices." Clearly the Eskimos had a different notion of the anthropologist, but nevertheless one I had to cope with.

Finally I explained that I was going to Tulugak Lake to map and excavate the locations that the young men had lived in during the seasonal rounds of 1947–48, the year Ingsted had lived with them, the year for which there was good "historical documentation." My plan was simple. Ingsted had visited the Nunamiut while they were still fully mobile hunters. He had described his experiences with these people. I wanted to view them archaeologically for the same time period so that some equations could be made between what a group looks like when viewed archaeologically and ethnographically. The almost universal response to my plan is typified by a response from Ben Ahgook, "Ingsted is not all true—he made some of it up." I pressed for clarification—"Oh he made it sound too much like 'old timers.'" I questioned on the subject of Ingsted's book many times and gradually a pattern emerged. The men agreed that Ingsted's writings made "it sound too much like old timers," and he had overdramatized the uncertainty of the hunting way of life. A frequent response was "Ingsted made it sound like the caribou didn't come—they did and things weren't so bad that winter as he said." Was it true that I couldn't trust the most relevant historical source?

Living in the village those first weeks convinced me that although the old men had remarkable memories for certain features of their past, my questions on the details of processing and disposal of caribou parts generally prompted responses such as "Eskimos use all the parts of the caribou." My best strategy would be to excavate the sites documented for the 1947–48 seasonal cycle so I could question them from a perspective of known characteristics of their sites. The archaeological data would provide the basis for the best interrogation strategy. If I could show them the concrete results of their behavior they would certainly be able to tell me what that behavior had been. Moving from the village to Tulugak Lake where we would begin archaeological investigations became a goal with a "promised land" kind of aura. We moved to Tulugak.

Johnny Rulland had gone with us as our guide and informant since he had lived at Tulugak in 1948. As I grew to know him better, his baseball cap and cast off military pants disturbed me less.

We worked hard recording and mapping the locations where the Nunamiut had lived during the summer of 1947 and summer and fall of 1948. Johnny remembered where every house had been, who had lived there, how long they had stayed and many other details. Working with him was a pleasure and he was a remarkable man when it came to memory of the terrain, locations of things, and the details of manufacturing different items. However, questioning him on the significance of variability in anatomical parts was rather unsatisfactory. He never seemed to understand what I was trying to learn. We worked hard, Johnny and I, and began the tedious job of collecting bone samples from the many houses we had mapped.

As this work proceeded and I learned more about methods of food preparation, little suggestive tidbits about drying meat, making rawhide rope, etc. I began to be anxious—there were so many things that seemed relevant as contributors to differing bone frequencies. How could I possibly get adequate control data?

As Johnny and I were collecting bones from around the telltale ring of stones where he and his father had camped in 1948, I noticed on an exposed rocky area a dense concentration of very tiny bone fragments. I asked Johnny what they had been doing that resulted in such a pile of tiny bones. He said "nothing—they must be from 'old timers.'" By this time knowledge about the "old timers" had become a goal since the contemporary setting was "so modern." We began to dig and with each tuft of tundra moss removed more bones in fascinating combinations and concentrations were exposed. A few flint chips appeared and we searched for the house we knew had to be there—all indications were that it was a winter occupation of some duration. We found the house and worked long hours on a site that was something of an archaeologist's dream. With every artifact discovered Johnny's eyes would light up and a detailed silent examination would follow with a statement, "This is a bird arrow, my father made one just like this for me when I was seven years old." He was interested and fascinated by what we were uncovering. This enthusiasm didn't extend, however, to my interest in the bones. I would ask, "Why are there nothing but metapodials in this pile?" Johnny's face would be almost a blank and finally he would say"I guess somebody was making akatuk." I quickly realized that Johnny, an Eskimo of forty years experience, who admittedly had seen or participated in practically every activity possibly represented on the site, was in the position of a very experienced archaeologist; he was making informed deductions. He was never willing to say for certain what the behavioral context had been for the patterns we observed. At best he would offer informed guesses. I was certainly glad to have his opinions, in most cases I think he was correct, but this was a far cry from the kind of "control" data I wanted to "explain" the observed variability in anatomical parts. While in the field I didn't let this stop me; we excavated with fascination and enthusiasm. Everything was recorded, plotted, measured—archaeologically the site and its documentation was truly extraordinary. There was a high yield of artifacts, nothing had been disturbed, and the fauna was magnificent.

I returned to the village carrying protectively the collection of artifacts, bones, and the crucial distribution maps of the bones. The most obvious forms of patterning at the site were in the bones; almost each artifact was unique and analogous forms were rarely present. The word about our work had preceded us and the old men were clearly fascinated and interested in seeing what we had found. Interviews were set

up and I began interrogations of the old men in terms of the concrete archaeological facts. The results were fascinating. Arctic John, Paneack, or Kakinya would sit with a bone arrow in their hands, a smile on their faces, and sometimes point out the most minute detail, talking of its meaning and frequently relating a series of personal experiences or experiences related to them by their fathers, relevent to the particular artifact which they held almost reverently. Such interest was not however uniformly expressed with respect to all the artifacts. They would paw through the box ignoring some, picking them up and tossing them back finally selecting one and smiling. This behavior annoyed me since each artifact was of equal value to me. Each artifact represented to me potentially new and different kinds of information about the past; each was a component of an assemblage. To understand the assemblage as a whole I needed information of equal detail on each different form.

I changed the manner of interviewing, keeping the assemblage hidden and producing an artifact at a time. This procedure worked better but still it was clear that the old men became bored quickly with some artifacts putting them down during my questioning and leaning over toward the box asking, "What else you got in there?" My disillusionment reached its highest peak when I attempted to question them about the most common item on the site—the bones. The men would look at the maps discussing in some detail the house remains, the hearth, and even spotting such details as where the dogs must have been, but when questioned about the patterning exhibited by the bones and different anatomical parts the common response was "I don't know, I guess they just put them that way." They were as surprised and more baffled by the bone data than I was, yet it was a way of life that they had experienced that had produced the distributions—why weren't they aware of them? I would press with more information about the bones and they would sit listening to some detail of association of frequency variation and respond "crazy Eskimoes."

Some said they would ask their wives, because after all the women did the cooking and taking out of trash. I set up interviews with two of the older women in the community. I went through the artifacts with them and noticed immediately a very different pattern of response. When showed the assemblage they would choose very different artifacts and express the same kind of nostalgic reminiscences over items which in many cases the men had largely ignored except when prompted by me. Clearly what was being played out in front of me was a different "value system" but it was not to be understood by the mere recognition of it in those terms. What I was witnessing was the expression of differential meaning being attached to the same objects clearly as a differential extension of self identities. I was administering a kind of artifactual Rorschach test. I was fascinated and spent much time trying to isolate the characteristics in terms of which common evaluations were being manifest by the choice sequences. In this I think I have been fairly successful. In spite of the fascination with the artifacts I shifted my work with the women onto the subject of the bones with high hopes. They saw different things in the patterning, asked questions of me, but were in general no more informative than the men.

I returned to New Mexico excited by the site, the knowledge gained about the artifacts, and impressed with the "old people." Charles Amsden remained in the village to collect information about group composition and settlement patterns from the old men. He had the additional charge to record in detail the activities of the hunting during the fall migration of caribou. As his data was mailed down to me piece by piece, my disappointment with the modern conditions in the village faded into the background. He was describing hunting, butchering, caching, and transporting of caribou parts. His statistics on the killing of males versus females matched almost exactly my statistics from the kill site survey. I was excited again about the bone data. It was not until over a year later that I had the opportunity of revisiting the Nunamiut.

I left New Mexico in April of 1971 excited by the prospects of observing them during the spring hunt and collecting data comparable to that already on hand for the fall hunt of 1969. As I stepped off the plane into the forty-two below

zero temperature I WAS SHOCKED ANEW. The same people were there to meet the plane but this time the modern world seemed remote. Caribou skin parkas were everywhere, the baggy caribou skin pants on some of the men seemed to roll and flair to the sides making them appear rounded and capable of bouncing if dropped. A sled and dog team were at the plane to carry the mail to the post office. In addition to the seeming remoteness of the modern world compared to my summer experience there were other surprises. Trails through the village familiar from my summer experiences were covered or blocked by huge snow drifts and winter sled trails wove through the village in a very different network.

There were marked differences in the social atmosphere. During summer the young men had hung around the village seemingly bored and idling away their time. Now they were so active it was difficult to find them. Everyday they were out with the dog team or snow-mobile "checking traps"—"looking for caribou"—"bringing in firewood"—"hauling water." On the other hand the women who had been so obvious during summer, as well as the old men, were rarely seen outside. In summer, the complaints commonly voiced were about how hot it was, the mosquitoes, and the behavior of the young people. Now all one heard from the women and aged was how bored they were and how they looked forward to summer. The hunters on the other hand complained of the absence of game, the fact that the caribou were late and the behavior of their dog teams or snow machines. How different things were. Suppose I had only records of a summer experience!

I stayed with Johnny and told him from the start that I didn't really want to talk to the old men; I wanted to do as many things with him and his age mates as possible so I could get some idea of what it was like hunting and trapping. He reacted with great enthusiasm and most of my time with the Nunamiut during that short experience was spent on a sled in temperatures which never got above eighteen degrees below zero.

It was during this period that I realized the information I wanted was right before my eyes in the form of the contemporary patterns of land use and variability in the activities at numerous locations still regularly used by the Nunamiut. They were still hunting caribou, still setting up hunting camps, still differentially treating caribou in terms of numerous conditions of temperature, number killed at once, location of kill, distance of transport, etc. My experience in winter hunting camp verified that the elusive differential distributions of parts of caribou were still being produced by the Nunamiut although they were not totally aware of it themselves. In this setting Johnny observed with me the high frequency of lower front leg bones on the winter hunting camp; he along with me became fascinated to discover how many different patterns there were and why they were different. His interest was never as intense as mine, but he recognized the problem and frequently guided me into situations which I would never have thought to investigate.

When I returned the following June with a large crew of students I saw in them surprise at the "modern" character of the village. They voiced their lack of understanding for my interest in the modern sites by tactfully pointing out the "really interesting" old timers' site nearby. That summer I collected a body of control data which began to yield the secrets of the patterning observable among anatomical parts. It was collected from the contemporary activities of the Nunamiut using guns, snowmobiles, etc. and they were much more surprised by its presence than I was. The dimensions, in terms of which contingent behavior operates, must be relevant to my Neanderthal data although the concrete behavior was certainly different.

Perhaps my initial disdain of the appearance of modernity reflects a bias by archaeologists as to the "relevance" of historically recent case material. Similarly my "discovery" of its "relevance" is something which "historical archaeologists" need to discover.

This was historical archaeology in the best sense of the word since I had available the best possible sources of information in addition to the archaeological record regarding past behavior—in many cases the persons who in fact had been responsible for the production of the archaeological record. Further, I had written documentation by both Ingsted and Gubser surviving about the past which I wished to investigate. Why were the details of this research not presented at a conference on "historical archaeology?" Was it because I was not interested in reconstructing the sites I had worked? Perhaps it was because persons living in the sites or the events occurring there were not considered historically "important" by contemporary American standards? Or maybe the questions I was asking and the approaches I used to gain answers would not be considered interesting or appropriate. After all, my interest in the Nunamiut did not stem from some abiding commitment to Eskimos or even their history. It arose out of a concern with explaining observed variability in the archaeological record as observed in Mousterian materials a continent away and separated from the Nunamiut by at least 60,000 years. I was interested in controlling variables so that their operation in determining observed distributions in the archaeological record could be evaluated, and meaning in processual terms could be given to what was observed. In short I chose to work with the Nunamiut because of the relevance of their situation for furthering the science of archaeology—not because of their "historical importance." Finally my primary interest was in a class of material—bones—about which historical accounts were mute and even the men who produced the patterns were unaware of their existence and meaning. This was an archaeological problem.

If we in discussion can answer the question as to why the results of my Nunamiut research were not considered by me to be appropriate to a conference on "historical archaeology," we may each gain a better understanding of the potential information to be gained from research by archaeologists on historically documented materials.

Department of Anthropology
University of New Mexico—Albuquerque

Bibliography

BINFORD, LEWIS R. AND SALLY R. BINFORD
1966 A preliminary analysis of functional variability in the Mousterian of Levallois facies. *American Anthropologist* 68 (2), pt. 2:238–295.

BORDES, F. H.
1961 Mousterian cultures in France. *Science* 134: 803–810.
1968 *The Old Stone Age*. World University Library, New York and London.

DIBBLE, DAVID S. AND DESSAMAE LORRAIN
1968 Bonfire Shelter: a stratified bison kill site, Val Verde County, Texas. *Texas Memorial Paper*, Miscellaneous Paper, No. 1.

GUBSER, NICHOLAS J.
1965 *The Nunamiut Eskimos: hunters of caribou*. Yale University Press, New Haven.

INGSTED, HELGE
1954 *Nunamiut*. Allen and Unwin, London.

KEHOE, THOMAS F.
1967 Boarding school bison drive site. *Plains Anthropologist*, Memoir Number 4.

WHITE, THEODORE E.
1954 Observations on the butchering technique of some aboriginal peoples, papers 3, 4, 5, 6. *American Antiquity* 19 (3): 254–264.

WOOD, RAYMOND E.
1962 Notes on bison bone from the Paul Brave, Huff and Demery sites (Oahe Reservoir). *Plains Anthropologist* 7: 201–204.

Archaeology and Folklore:
Common Anxieties,
Common Hopes

Henry Glassie

OURS IS AN UNCOMMON ENCOUNTER. In the United States, folklorists do not frequently address assemblies of archaeologists. That is a strange state of affairs. In Europe, the folklorist has long studied the artifact, and, though the American folklorist's attentiveness to artifactual information is recent, it is currently strong and intense. If the archaeologist does not dig, or the folklorist does, our pursuits verge near identity. It is not the shared interest in the artifact which makes the lack of shared communication odd, however. It is odd because folklore and archaeology are paradigmatically quite similar disciplines with much to give and gain in a closer association.

During the nineteenth century, folklorists and archaeologists joined anthropologists in the attempt to reconstitute the unwritten past by the examination of survivals. The twentieth century found anthropologists hastily building, then savagely destroying a series of flamboyant theories, while folklorists and archaeologists patiently constructed humble methodologies. We regularized the collecting and ordering of information in a manner that bore a truthful relation to our traditional objects of study. We achieved descriptive precision, and developed a deep neurosis: theory envy.

After the field report, what? In their separate, but equally well-built and organized disciplines, modern folklorists and archaeologists knuckle their heads and wonder.

Our questioning, our parallel successes and failures, arise naturally from the deepest of our similarities. Both of our disciplines have wings clearly situated in the humanities and in the social sciences. There are literary folklorists and anthropological folklorists, just as there are classical archaeologists and anthropological archaeologists. Both disciplines are united by field method and sundered by interpretive orientation. It looks as though schizophrenia is the diagnosis.

In each of our disciplines there have been important recent attempts to purify research. Our immediate histories have been marked by works successfully promising new perspectives. Parricidal tendencies have been unleashed, crises of self-hate and hope have broken over us, and yet there is an undercurrent of resistance to the acculturation of our study to some other. The image of science looms aloof, pristinely, admirably. We accept its ascendency, yet remain unwilling to follow it, if following means the amputation of our social responsibilities and humane sensibilities. We want to be scientists, for the scientist works with care and honesty, but would the full acceptance of a scientific program force us to abandon profundity for efficiency? There are problems without solutions, hypotheses that are untestable, realities measureless to man. The great enduring problems of existence, the matters that matter, can be approached with care and honesty, but they are not available to experimentation, to hypothetico-deductive structuring or to nomothetic reduction. The scientist becomes embarrassed and cowers behind method when asked a question like the meaning of life.

Novelists offer answers to the big ones—life, death, happiness, reason, will. But we correctly distrust the arrogant subjectivity of the novelist as much as we do the gutless objectivity of the scientist. And our disciplines remain sited directly over the fault on the academic landscape that separates the social sciences from the humanities. This situation is the source of our confusion and our strength. Archaeology and folklore are the only disciplines with such an exquisitely central site. We should not have to go through the sort of schismatic reinvention that is current in anthropology. We can harken simultaneously to the wispy but profound messages wafting over from the humanities and to the orderly, if sometimes trivial, messages that march in from the social sciences. We can give our attention at once to the humanist's concern for meaning, intention, and being, and to the scientist's concern for form, behavior, and conditions. When we can test, count, and answer, we must; but when we cannot, we need not despair; we can engage in discourse, in orderly, open, scientific discussion about the nature of humanity.

There are other interesting comparisons between your study and mine, details to uncover and catalog, but more exact analogizing would be presumptuous, so I will turn to a little account of folklore's present state. I do this, however, knowing that the similarities between archaeology and folklore are various and numerous. I use writings by James Deetz and Lewis Binford in my graduate classes in "folklore theory." My description, then, may claim the virtues of a parable in this context.

In their studies, lined with collectanea and indexes, folklorists fidget in angst. Their lineage begins with the great romantics, but for some reason this embarrasses them. Like others with a social scientific bent, they refer most readily to the rationalists and scientists in their collective past; despite historic truths, their myths are peopled by Comte not Rousseau, Darwin not Ruskin, Radcliffe-Brown not Yeats. Growing afraid of grand schemes and big thoughts of unbridled brilliance, their recent forebears became content to while years away in classifying and annotating the shards of wit and scraps of ancient poesy they had dug up. For many, the field report was sufficient. Others reassembled the collected scraps in chronological order to create histories—not histories of people, but histories of things, such as folktales or pottery.

Enough of this, cried a new and self-consciously professional generation almost exactly a decade ago. Modernism, the half-century old search for the abstractly principled, had, at last, battered its way into folkloristic awareness. The message of Kandinsky, Einstein, Joyce, Freud, Wittgenstein, and de Saussure had arrived. Unclearly. It was felt first as a vague malaise, a curious discomfort like a lad's first hangover. The symptoms were enraged rejection, exhibited in attacks on all that their elders held dear, and an immediate urge to steal any unprotected intellectual treasure in academe.

The new generation's first ideas were those to

which folklorists had already laid some claim. Initially, their revolution was modest and amounted mostly to the expansion of their study domain in two directions. Instead of studying only oral items, the folklorist could study the behavioral contexts in which the items were naturally performed. In archaeology, this would be comparable to studying the site as a systemic whole, rather than as a congeries of components. The old folklorists had considered such possibilities, but only haphazardly. Instead of studying only traditional literature, the folklorist could now study traditional actions and artifacts too. In archaeology, this would be comparable to studying artifacts found above ground level as well as below. European scholars had been doing this all along, Americans had suggested the possibility for years, but the concerted study of what became known as "folklife" was a novelty.

The new folklorists seemed healthy, but nonetheless fretful. They brooded in envy of the urbanities of academe, uncomfortable in the old role of hunter and gatherer, contemplating the sins of their past, codifying their discipline in a mound of textbooks that rose around them, and scanning the horizon for help. The most venturesome stole quietly away and spied on the anthropologists, who were spying on the linguists, who were spying on the physicists, who were reading Blake.

It was, the sixties, a time of general intellectual unhappiness. The Western cosmos had changed shape (around 1910), modern times had come and gone, and scholars, it seems, were about the last to hear about it. Folklorists did try to catch up. Some labored to formalize field methods, to make our hunting, already quite careful and not unscientific, more rigorous in order to differentiate the professional from the mere pot hunter. Sharpening the tools in our old field kits was hardly enough, so others became theory thieves, taking Dell Hymes' constructs and replacing the word "sentence" with "folktale" or "I house." It is wholly natural, as Thomas Kuhn has shown, for scholars, itchy for progress during times of crisis, to import concepts from other disciplines. But it did begin to appear that folklore could become reformulated as a shadow of anthropology. Perhaps the

new folklore was only the old anthropology. The proud new essays, glistening with the appellation "theoretical," were mostly logical exercises and bibliographic surveys. They proved that folklorists, too, could talk that talk. These essays served to rid the discipline of the last of the old amateurs. They wrecked our prose style. They made us think.

Some traditionalists rejected the new theorizing, though they were hard-pressed to say why—it seems to have been something about keeping the faith and preventing the neighborhood from going to hell. But, the new savants had gained the center of the stage. The spotlights played on them; their colleagues rendered them a respectful, attentive silence. Silence. They seemed to have little to say.

The field methods were in order. Anyone, for instance, who studied folk artifacts (old buildings, mostly), had read all the prescriptive statements by cultural geographers, historians, archaeologists, and design theorists. Things were comprehensively and carefully measured, sited, quantified. The theories seemed to be in order. Folklorists prowled the bookstores at the beginning of each semester and found out what they were reading in anthropology, psychology, sociology, and linguistics, and read it too. Still, there was little joy in the folklorists' encampment.

All the time they had been gazing toward the more scientific disciplines, behind them languished, unexamined, the reasons why all these ballads or communication events or barns were getting studied in the first place.

The crucial problem lay not in method nor in theory but in the relation between them. That, it is important to mark, is a point of difference between our disciplines. In archaeology, the anthropological theorists have consistently related their thought to empirical realities. Jim Deetz and Lew Binford have muddied their boots as well as worked their brains. In folklore, some are doing tight, scientific fieldwork (though "some" means few nowadays), and others are orating insightfully and logically about "theory," but there is little rapport between these halves of the discipline, even when they appear within the same individual. We talk about symbolic interaction, behaviorism, structuralism, but almost none of us are using data to refine theory or theory to explain data.

A resolution of the dilemma begins to emerge when we recognize that the social scientists who developed the theories that folklorists coveted and stole did so in terms of a tradition incorporating norms of study object and goal as well as methods and theories. We have study objects. I like old houses. We have favorite theories. I like structuralism. But if I, unthinkingly, perform a structural analysis of old houses, or an interactional analysis of jokes, all I have done is amuse myself, no matter how careful I was in the field, no matter how fully I comprehended the relevant theoretical literature.

I will leave it to you to decide how smoothly the comparisons between our disciplines continue here, but I think that folklorists are currently unhappy and incapable of nice synthesis in the dialectic of the empirical and the theoretical because they have neglected to examine their goals with the same care they have applied to their field methods and theories. And it is precisely the goals, the ultimate purposes for study, that guide the interrelation of study object and theory.

Whether or not folklore has been successful in pulling itself together, it remains true of folklore, as it is true of archaeology, that its central position on the academic landscape provides its practitioners with great potential for mental integration. As I write, I have before me not only a scratchy draft of the paper I planned to give at the pleasant and stimulating meeting in Charleston, but as well, memories of the rant I actually presented. At this point in the oral performance I announced that I was one of folklore's scientizers. I have written some of folklore's most careful, quantified, and boring studies. For a while I wished to purge folklore in imitation of the best anthropology, but now, I am glad that never happened. I like folklore's dangerous location on that fault separating the sciences from the humanities. Here, somehow the image of the Delphic Oracle blundered into my brain. I thought of her, seated over a fissure in the ground, sniffing the fumes that rose from it, and offering grand pronouncements. I like breathing in the mixed air of this academic border country. That is not because I wish to indulge in unrestrained, intuitive singing. It is because we scholars are as much the products of history and immediate conditions as the people we study. The sciences and the humanities are only cultural conventions, directions not places; their separation is a convenient but false dichotomy like the abstract versus the real, the objective versus the subjective, the theoretical versus the empirical, the deductive versus the inductive. We cannot study without having our thought affected by our feelings, our feelings affected by art and social need. Nor can our studies exist without consequences. "Pure" scientists who manipulate data, atoms, or DNA molecules without awareness of the influences on their thought and the implications of their acts are deluding themselves and unwittingly participating in a modern dance of death. Humanists who manipulate words and logics without regard for the real progress of scientific thought are similarly deluded, if less immoral. Since we are Western people, when we study people, we cannot help but be both scientist and humanist. It is wiser for us to be conscious of this duality, to control it and use it for good ends, than it is for us to pretend to purity. Purity exists only in the realm of the supernatural. Pure science is modern superstition.

All disciplines devoted to understanding man display both scientific and humanistic tendencies. In folklore (and I feel in archaeology) our methods and theories come most naturally from the social sciences, but our goals come most naturally from the humanities. Our careful work must teach us something about volitional, angelic animals. We want to do the impossible and do it well.

To be serious in our studies, we must work rigorously and argue clearly. We must be scientists. Once scientists studied natural phenomena as evidence of a divine intelligence. Now they study natural phenomena as evidence of natural laws. Having murdered God, they can have no teleology, but social scientists have one whether they want it or not: there is nothing mystically medieval about imputing will to human beings; cultural phenomena make no sense unless they are studied as evidence of the existence of a worldly intelligence. Our goal is forming a theory of mind. Science for science's sake, like art for art's sake, is a decadent, dishonest game. The purpose of our science is to help us draw as full a picture as possible of the actuality and potential of humanity. A limited picture of man as tool maker or social animal or speaker or nay-sayer will not do. Only a full picture will aid in the development of priorities for study. All things are not equally important; some very careful research is a waste of time, a parody of methodology. Only a full picture will help us, as people, approach happiness and perfection. The reason for our science is to make us good humanists. The reason for humanism is to make us good scientists. The reason for our study is to make us good people.

So, here we are, perched on our oracular stools, filling our lungs with strange air, and becoming a bit nauseous. When we took in the theories of the more positivistic scientists, we also took in, unawares, their goals, and these blended badly with those of our tradition. As presently practised, behavioral, positivistic, social science enslaves the people we wish to understand, reducing them to rats and factors, and it enslaves us, preventing us from commenting on central issues, such as individual will and the collective quality of life, and consigning us to orderly argument about peripheral matters, such as social organization and architectural forms. If the archaeologist or the folkloristic student of artifacts were to accept the positivistic constraints of, say, cinematographic students of kinesics, we would record and code our objects with great care. We would have done things "scientifically," but at the end of our labors, all we would have would be descriptions, excellently correlated descriptions, of old junk. A full description of a nonverbal interchange is interesting because we impute motives to the actors, but a full description of the pot shards dug out of a hole is interesting only to the few specialists who can inwardly restore some human sense to them.

Explanation is our mode. The way to explanation is through the coordination of theories with study objects and field methods on one hand, with goals and philosophical methods on the other. I want now to consider the interrelated problems of object selection and goal orientation that folklorists and archaeologists share.

The positivistic brand of social science provides special problems for us students of artifacts. Since we have been taught that it is the outer world which counts, that behavior not thought is our object, much clever speculation has been devoted to reconstructing the uses of old things. I remember hearing a paper at an S.H.A. meeting in Pennsylvania, the author of which opined that the numerous wine bottles recovered from privies were used for female masturbation. That is an engaging notion and we could play with it for hours, but such thoughts are always difficult to offer with conviction and they always lead to the writing of a fiction—historical short stories. It is both more profound and theoretically easier to read an artifact first as the end product of a mental process of design, as a projection of thought rather than as an element in performance, as an expression of cognitive pattern rather than a reflection of behavioral pattern. In short, I want to see the artifact as cultural, not material.

It is a fine pastime to mull over the uses of old artifacts, but the theorist of use would learn most quickly and efficiently in situations involving live people. If we choose to begin with the artifact, then our first goal should be the attempt to face the thing, not as a usable entity or a mere object, but as a sign, as the result of an intention. However it was used, the artifact was the largely unconscious realization and materialization of a mental dynamic.

Antonin Artaud talks about the gods asleep in jade in museums. In prison. Our goal, says he, is releasing the spirit of the gods so we can use that spirit to regenerate ourselves. Less poetically, our purpose is developing the ability to see, to experience form as the product of a mental argument over order. Still more directly, the object we select for study must be theorized as the result of the employment of mental rules for right form.

Anything human beings do can be examined in this way, the way Burke uses to understand literature, the way Chomsky uses to understand sentences, but why do we choose artifacts over other things?

Any principle that can be developed in the

27

human sciences could be developed first by an archaeologist. There are no absolute limits to an archaeologist's nomothetic intentions or serendipitous discoveries, but some of the patterns we need to discover require the use of artifacts (as opposed to using artifacts because we chance to like them). These are patterns in time. The study of artifacts is a most roundabout way to come to an understanding of many aspects of culture, and many problems would be most efficiently left to ethnographers. But if our worries have a temporal dimension (and unless we are content with tautological "models," they do), then we must consider the artifact.

Time. The personality of past periods. Principles of culture change. Time is the reason for artifactual study, and understanding history— the mutability of mind—is a goal folklorists and archaeologists share. We know that people change profoundly from time to time. We know that, mythically and really, the past impinges dreadfully upon the present.

Some of the new folklorists have tried to kill time. The survivalists, evolutionists, and historic-geographic diffusionists were concerned with history. They are out of fashion. The flashy social scientists that folklorists want to emulate seem to be uninterested in history, so, though it means the loss of one major motivation for folkloristic study, and though it means the acceptance of static, politically conservative conceptualizations, folklorists are adopting the presentistic perspective.

There are different reasons for the elimination of time in the recent past of anthropology. One is that historical and ethnological facts drop out of sight and importance when the search is for human universals. Still, the artifact, historic and prehistoric, could be used as proof or disproof of a universal logic. The other reason is that the social anthropologists of the thirties seemed to have had no history to study. Their positivism instructed them to consider only sensate phenomena. The exotic people they chose to bother lacked writing and sometimes archaeological depth. We can profit from them, for it is epistemologically essential to create the kind of synchronic models they strove to produce. But, unlike them, we need

not stop there. Synchrony is but a step toward diachrony. It is always possible to gain some feeling for the antecedents of a synchronic model from archaeology, oral tradition, or the early comments of outsiders, but it is not always possible to study diachronically. If two, temporally separated systems cannot be constructed and compared, then obviously the student has to stop with synchrony. But students of artifacts need not: they can build the junk of different strata into principled structures and then contrast them.

We are ready to pose the question again: why do we choose to study the artifact?

Some artifacts seem to be interesting in themselves because they are beautiful or because they exist in sets. People like to dig them up and measure them. People like to order them and save them. Psychologists should study people of this sort and people of this sort should write about themselves as a contribution to a phenomenology of fascination. Folklorists and archaeologists study artifacts to learn about people, other people and themselves. Our job is not easy.

Generally artifacts are poor in content. Compare the immanent richness of a clay pipe with that of a High Mass. Generally artifacts do not vary sensitively with their conditions. Compare the flexibility of a house with that of a conversation. Artifacts are less delicately expressive and reflective than most modes of human communication. Were we to accept the development of synchronous systems as an end goal along with other fashionable anthropologica, there would be little reason to analyze artifacts. If you wish to know, abstractly, about social mechanisms, you will learn more in a few weeks of observing people than you will in years of measuring pots or houses. If you wish to know the nature of mental operations, you will find it more profitable to study people who can talk than things which cannot. But when your wish is to understand people who are dead, artifacts are all you have. They last.

We share the goal of the comprehension of the variation of intentions in time. The artifact is the only study object we can choose. Some of these artifacts have writing on them, and so long as we are willing to study the literate, the wealthy and the maladjusted, we can begin our study with artifacts like novels, autobiographies, and diaries. If we are concerned with the endless silent majority who did not leave us written projections of their minds (and only a person's own expressions are useful if we admit to the overpowering importance of the unconscious), then we are left with the study of mute artifacts like old houses, busted pots, and projectile points.

Because of his commitment to the primacy of print, the historian has been unable to produce an authentic history. As folklorists and historical archaeologists, one of our tasks is to rescue from anonymity the average people of the past. Our role is not humbly complementary. We should not stand at the service of the priests of the written record. It is superficial and elitist—a tale of viciousness, a myth for the contemporary power structure. Writing cannot be used to form the democratic, projective, quantifiable base for the study of past people. Artifacts can.

One major rationale for artifactual analysis is the creation of a record of what folks were thinking, dull or exciting, during that vast time out of mind. The present and very recent past would be most efficiently left to ethnographers and oral historians, for they will get more out of people than we will out of things. Of course you need not call in another researcher—those are easy, pleasant jobs; I have done them both—you need only to remember to talk with people when you can. Once students of ethnography, oral tradition, and mute artifacts have established a new chronicle, then we can ask those who like to understand the past via subliterature to provide us with anecdotes and cooperate with us in the development of explanations for the chronicle's patterning.

We have a goal: recording the shifts in cognition over time in order to create an authentic history. We have a study object: mute artifacts. Our goals and objects are nicely related. It might seem that all artifacts are of value and all sites are worth digging. That may be so, but some artifacts and sites are of much greater importance than others, depending upon whether we choose to work at history in a particularistic or a universalistic manner.

The particularistic historians' purpose is im-

proving the understanding of the past of a given people or place. When they elect to work within this frame, students of artifacts will find it easy to make their findings relevant. The wonderful study of Johnny Ward's ranch had an accidental genesis. The dig taught nothing about the historical interests which sent archaeologists to the site, but because we all have some feeling for the conventions of American historiography, the quick glimpses it gives us of Johnny and his pigeon-toed lady are treasures of inestimable worth. As a folklorist, as the academic friend of men like Johnny Ward, I am grateful.

Particularistic history consists of the correlation of sequential ethnographies. Although any dig might contribute to this vertical ethnology, we already have constructs named history which can suggest to us priorities of need. I would generalize that our greatest lack—within the ambit of European-American historiography—lies in the era spanned by the second to fourth generations in any occupance, and among the people of the working class. The initial settlers sometimes left reports. The later inhabitants are still remembered. Rich people hired clever people to write about themselves and the quaintness of the poorest people. The person we do not know at all is the farmwife on a nonslaveholding Piedmont seat of 1810. If we can accumulate enough portraits of times and places, carefully chosen to stop the largest lacunae in our ignorance, we might be able to offer a compassionate, accurate alternative to the historian's account. Shreds and patches, to be sure, but sewn as honestly as we can do it.

The other historical goal, universalizing and law tending, would direct us to use artifacts to develop increasingly better theories of human thought and action in time. There is no end to the possible principled statements about patterns of stasis and change, just as there is no end to the sites waiting to be dug. Since the task is endless, it would be wise to consider which of the principles that could be built out of artifactual evidence we most need to know.

Not all principles and laws are of equal value. Interesting ones are more valuable than dull ones. Interesting ones that hold relevance for our comprehension of modern existence are more valuable than interesting ones which do not. It is strange to be saying this, but many modern scholars think solving any petty deductive puzzle is worth their time. Just because things can be counted, does not mean they should be. Just because some idea can be framed as a hypothesis, does not mean it should be tested. The conclusion that can be predicted with certainty is not worth study.

Of greatest importance, I would say, are studies which assist us in understanding the evolution of alienation. There are few places on the globe that could not offer us valuable data, though some times and places seem most crucial: northern France in the eleventh century, northern Italy in the fourteenth, the English Midlands in the sixteenth, the west of Ireland in the nineteenth, the interior of Brazil in the twentieth. Turning to North America, I feel the times most deserving of examination and contemplation during our quest for self-knowing are: the moment of initial European occupance everywhere, when the land was broken; the period 1730–1765 along the Eastern seaboard, when, it appears, the classic American syndrome of courageous intolerance was set; the period 1900–1915 between the Alleghenies and the Rockies, when we lost control of our destinies. The above-ground artifacts I study suggest that other times were filled with adjusting to, and exploring the implications of, the revolutions that took place then.

Reversing from effect to plausible cause, I think that the moments when a society shifts its economic base should call the archaeologist (or the ethnographer) to them. What happens when capitalism comes and goes, anywhere, anytime?

Suppose now we have developed an interesting historical question—particularistic or universalistic—and selected a good site in which to explore or test our driving idea. Depending upon the amount we already know, we can call this idea a hypothesis or admit it is only an a priori guide. Hypotheses too rapidly and trimly formed will nearly guarantee triviality. Guiding notions left unexamined and unformulated will nearly guarantee futility. Suppose then we have recorded the site's artifacts and the multiplex empirical relations between them. The theoretical tie that will bind our historical idea—

our goal—to our material will not, as intellectual history proves, just emerge.

Whatever our goals, we begin by studying objects. One of the traits our disciplines share is, though we are aware of institutions and cultures and periods, we tend to build up to them through the careful examination of small things—sites and artifacts, contexts and texts—rather than accepting large unknowns as givens. We start modestly, precisely with real phenomena, with relatively autonomous study objects.

Our theory, our mechanism of interpretation, must be constructed to order the discrete things we start with, breaking them down to build them up into larger and larger systems. These systems will be of two, interpenetrating sorts: one, formal and reductive, derived through analysis; one, signifying and expansive, derived through analogy. Since the most fashionable references for those who attempt such work are to linguistics, it seems natural for us to name these planes of the artifactual phenomenon "syntax" and "semantics." Many who employ such comparisons do so only because they are in vogue. Others feel that comparing their efforts with those of modern linguists will genuinely power better thought. The reason that linguistics, or, more broadly, the range of contemporary thinking subsumed by the label structuralism, is fashionable and contains force for anyone attempting to understand mind by arranging human expressions into systems is that it is the latest, clearest formulation of a long tradition of Western thought on just that matter: how facts can be systematized, comprehensibly and meaningfully.

Whether we refer deeply into our philosophical great tradition, or, more shallowly, to the structuralist program developed out of it, our first theoretical problem is formal. The linguistic research most useful for us (since we deal with structures for which no meanings are obvious) is that of pure transformational syntax, the early hermetic models of Noam Chomsky, for instance. Although it would have been difficult to imagine without him, old formalistic or recent phenomenological procedures might also have suggested that our theory's first task is to provide a description of form in terms of the relational rules required for its complete design. What the thing is—that is but a matter of measurement. It is a rock of a certain size and sort, with a certain shape, a certain number of notches. Nothing theoretical there. What theory needs to tell us is how the thing came to be. Not how it was made. But how it was thought. What were the rules in its designer's mind? There is no way to prove or disprove the reality of these "rules." They are theoretical, an attempt to state the unknown in a logical manner. The best we can do is to write the rules into a parsimonious, closed system, in which every rule is bound to every rule. The system is a theory of design, leading from simple, powerful essences—pure geometric images, in the case of artifacts—to complex, real things.

Things have been surrendered to process. At the end of the first phase in our performance of theory we will have not a chaotic collection of objects nor a rationalistic shopping list of items —the sort of enumeration the old folklorists and archaeologists produced—but a formal system. A grammar perhaps. At least it will be a statement similar to the syntactic component in a grammar interrelating all artifacts by means of a set of rules that account for the generation of their forms. Near the top of this system, we will have the artifactual types—complete structural abstractions of shape. Near its bottom will be the culture's formal essences. Between will run a program of transformations, rules providing the procedures by which the essences may be altered into types, the types into artifacts.

This system of rules will provide us with a complete statement of all the similarities and differences in a particular set of data. Instead of a few hundred things to study, we will have a hierarchical arrangement of thousands of facts. We have so little information from the past that we need to get as much as we can from each scrap that has tumbled down to us. But the information can get out of hand, so we must arrange it. Every artifact is the product of the employment of a great many mental rules, but each artifact will share rules to a greater or lesser extent with others. The degree of sharedness allows us to create a single statement in which some rules or sets of rules, such as those requiring symmetry, will appear to be especially com-

mon or fundamental. At the end of all this, we have a processual theory of form—an account of the composition of all the artifacts from the site to which our historical interests took us. And we are ready to go on to the next stage.

The theory's formal, analytic phase can be complete. The next one cannot be. Guided by the suggestions of transformational grammarians and axiomatic formalists we can create full theories of form. But there seems to be no way to account fully for meaning.

We Westerners are good at closed systems. The order science invents makes us happy. Disorder scares us. We try to escape reality by reducing it to models, by closing the open possibilities. Linguists have much more trouble with semantics than syntax. Once formalized as competence, syntax becomes a closed system using finite means to produce infinite results. Semantics seems to be an open system. That may be a contradiction—"open system"—and perhaps our very affection for systematics prevents us from developing a good theory for meaning. But it does seem that just as the artifact is the product of a structure of design, it is the vehicle for an orderly, if not exactly systematic, structure of analogy. This structure, this "open system," is the sort of mental construct Yeats called a phantasmagoria. It gives the artifact an infinite, but meaningful, referential potential.

The philosophical tradition that makes it easy to talk about the theory's initial analytic phase makes it difficult to talk about its second referential phase, but I have moved through both phases while forcing dumb old houses to speak historically, and though the second phase is difficult to outline methodically, it is not difficult to do. It involves the discovery of relations and regularities that obtain despite the rules, and levels of rules, that heave thought from the abstract toward the concrete. The formal analysis obliged us to adhere to the syntagmatic relations of the surface. Now we allow ourselves to rearrange reality, like a nonobjective painter or a *bricoleur*, and join the sundered aspects of form into paradigms. These paradigms may be reducible to essences—complementary to the formal essences—or they may be laterally or obliquely related into an endless stream of metamorphosis, after the manner of Lévi-Strauss.

Claude Lévi-Strauss is one of the few people in our academic neighborhood having the courage to work on an open system. He is misunderstood, dismissed as unrestrained. But meaning is no less real than form, it is just less accessible to our reductive scientistic procedures. He is working on a crucial matter as scientifically as possible. And he functions as the modern exemplar of the theory's second stage, much as Chomsky did of the first, though it is possible to find enough anticipation of his work in old philosophical writings to suggest, again, that it might have been done without him. He made it easier for us to approach the strangely ignored problem of meaning, but his mediated oppositions, endlessly flowing, are a modernist's version of our old ally, the dialectic.

To make sense of our site we needed only the artifacts and one additional fact: these things were made by people. We needed no speculative insights or ethnological analogies; all we did was describe things as the result of an interplay between closed formal structures and open affecting structures. Setting these structures of mind against human universals—matters like life and death, stranger and friend, hot and cold, tame and wild—we can arrive at a meaningful structure of a past culture. We have done what we can without referring outside of our site's confines.

We can stop there, but we do not have to. Our conclusions—the data compressed into powerful statements—are available for a great variety of comparative studies. There are other sites which can be built into comparable models. There are documents and ethnological findings with which comparison can be made in order to improve our understanding of a particular people or to aid in the development of generalizing statements. Our theory, that is, nicely articulated our ultimate historical goals with our original study objects.

The only limits to the theory's application are drawn by the data itself and the student's energy and wit. Despite their inherent weaknesses, artifacts can be transformed into a multitude of structures expressive of mind. The limits on comparative endeavors are drawn only by will and desire. The potential for correlation is boundless. We need, then, to know what we want to learn, and if we are sensitive to our data and to ourselves we will know. In general, we will wish to learn the personality of a past people whose existence holds implications for our own, or we will wish to discover some temporal principles that will help us comprehend our existence.

The past is too important to leave to historians. The human reality is too important to leave to novelists. We are the guardians and students of the objects which can provide modern people with their best entrance to history. And history is one of the best entrances to self awareness. We must be careful and introspective as the recent theorists have taught us to be, but we would be fools to chain our brains in an effort at artificial purity. Just because we adopt a rigorous method and an openly stated, logically formulated theory does not mean we cannot become emotionally involved in our work; it does not mean we have to shy from poetic and profound questions. Just because we wish to consider great human problems does not mean we cannot work with care and honesty. We can be serious, scientific scholars and still allow human beings their splendor and their stupidity. In fact, we cannot be serious and scientific if we do not.

The impure tradition we share, as archaeologists and folklorists, will enable us to free the people of the past from historiographic bondage, letting them live again truthfully. If we will only let it, our tradition will also enable us to free ourselves from dogmatic, scholastic inhibitions, so that we can pay constant attention to the reasons for our study, the objects we study, and the theories we use to relate our goals and objects, in order to fulfill ourselves as thinkers and human beings.

We share together the obligation to restore history to humanity and reason to scholarship.

Department of Folklore and Folklife
University of Pennsylvania

Bibliography

Most of the intellectual debts I incurred while developing this paper are too broad or too deep to be captured in scattered parenthetical citations. I list below the works that influenced me while I wrote and the works I intended, now coyly, now brashly, to refer you to.

ARMSTRONG, ROBERT PLANT
1971 *The affecting presence: an essay in humanistic anthropology*. University of Illinois Press, Urbana.

ARTAUD, ANTONIN
1958 *The theater and its double*, translated by Mary Caroline Richards. Grove Press, New York.

BARTHES, ROLAND
1970 *Elements of semiology*, translated by Annette Lavers and Colin Smith. Beacon Press, Boston.
1975 *The pleasure of the text*, translated by Richard Miller. Hill and Wang, New York.

BIDNEY, DAVID
1967 *Theoretical anthropology*. Schocken, New York.

BINFORD, SALLY R. and LEWIS R. (Editors)
1968 *New perspectives in archaeology*. Aldine, Chicago.

BIRDWHISTELL, RAY L.
1970 Kinesics and context: essays on body motion communication. *Conduct and Communication* 2. University of Pennsylvania Press, Philadelphia.

BLOCH, MARC
1953 *The historian's craft*, translated by Peter Putnam. Vintage Books, New York.

BOCHEŃSKI, J. M.
1968 *The methods of contemporary thought*, translated by Peter Caws. Harper and Row, New York.

BROWN, ROBERT
1963 *Explanation in social science*. Aldine, Chicago.

BURKE, KENNETH
1968 *Language as symbolic action: essays on life, literature and method*. University of California Press, Berkeley.
1969 *A grammar of motives*. University of California Press, Berkeley.
1973 *The philosophy of literary form*. University of California Press, Berkeley.

BUTTERFIELD, HERBERT
1965 *The Whig interpretation of history*. W. W. Norton, New York.

CHANG, K. C. (Editor)
1968 *Settlement archaeology*. National Press Books, Palo Alto.

CHOMSKY, NOAM
1957 Syntactic structures. *Janua Linguarum* 4. Mouton, The Hague.
1966 *Cartesian linguistics: a chapter in the history of rationalist thought*. Harper and Row, New York.
1970 *Aspects of the theory of syntax*. M. I. T. Press, Cambridge.

DEETZ, JAMES
1967 *Invitation to archaeology*. Natural History Press, Garden City.
1971 (Editor) *Man's imprint from the past: readings in the methods of archaeology*. Little, Brown, Boston.

DETHLEFSEN, EDWIN and JAMES DEETZ
1966 Death's heads, cherubs, and willow trees: experimental archaeology in colonial cemeteries. *American Antiquity* 31(4): 502–510.

DORSON, RICHARD M. (Editor)
1972 *Folklore and folklife: an introduction*. University of Chicago Press, Chicago.

EVANS, E. ESTYN
1973 *The personality of Ireland: habitat, heritage, and history*. Cambridge University Press, New York.
1975 Archaeology and folklife. *Béaloideas* 39–41:127–139.

FELD, STEVEN
1974 Linguistic models in ethnomusicology. *Journal of the Society for Ethnomusicology* XVIII(2):197–217.

FERNANDEZ, JAMES
1974 The mission of metaphor in expressive culture. *Current Anthropology* 15(2):119–145.

FISCHER, JOHN L.
1961 Art styles as cultural cognitive maps. *American Anthropologist* 63(1): 79–93.

FONTANA, BERNARD L.
1965 On the meaning of historic sites archaeology. *American Antiquity* 31 (1):61–65.
1968 Bottles, buckets, and horseshoes: the unrespectable in American archaeology. *Keystone Folklore Quarterly* XIII(3):171–184.
1973 The cultural dimensions of pottery: ceramics as social documents. In *Ceramics in America*, edited by Ian M. G. Quimby, pp. 1–13. University Press of Virginia for the Henry Francis duPont Winterthur Museum, Charlottesville.

FONTANA, BERNARD L. and J. CAMERON GREENLEAF, et al.
1962 Johnny Ward's ranch: a study in historic archaeology. *The Kiva* 28(1–2):1–115.

GLASSIE, HENRY
1969 Pattern in the material folk culture of the

eastern United States. *Folklore and Folklife* 1. University of Pennsylvania Press, Philadelphia.

1973 Structure and function, folklore and the artifact. *Semiotica* VIII(4):313–351.

1974 The variation of concepts in tradition: barn building in Otsego County, New York. In Man and cultural heritage: papers in honor of Fred Kniffen, edited by H. J. Walker and W. G. Haag. *Geoscience and Man* V:177–235. School of Geoscience, Louisiana State University, Baton Rouge.

1975a *Folk housing in middle Virginia: a structural analysis of historical artifacts*. University of Tennessee Press, Knoxville.

1975b *All silver and no brass: an Irish Christmas mumming*. Indiana University Press, Bloomington.

GOLDSTEIN, KENNETH S.
1964 *A guide for field workers in folklore*. Folklore Associates, Hatboro.

GREIMAS, A. JULIEN
1971 The interpretation of myth: theory and practice. In Structural analysis of oral tradition, edited by Pierre Maranda and Elli Köngäs Maranda. *Folklore and Folklife* 3: 81–121. University of Pennsylvania Press, Philadelphia.

HALL, ROBERT A. JR.
1972 Why a structural semantics is impossible. *Language Sciences* 21:1–6.

HANSEN, WILLIAM F.
1972 The conference sequence: patterned narration and narrative inconsistency in the Odyssey. *Classical Studies* 8. University of California Press, Berkeley.

HARRIS, MARVIN
1971 *The rise of anthropological theory: a history of theories of culture*. Thomas Y. Crowell, New York.

HYMES, DELL
1972 (Editor) *Reinventing anthropology*. Vintage Books, New York.

1975 Foundations in sociolinguistics: an ethnographic approach. *Conduct and communication*. University of Pennsylvania Press, Philadelphia.

JENKINS, J. GERAINT
1968 Post-Medieval archaeology and folklife studies. *Post-Medieval Archaeology* 2:1–9.

KANDINSKY, WASSILY
1964 Concerning the spiritual in art, translated by Michael Sadlier. *The Documents of Modern Art* 5. George Wittenborn, New York.

KING, ROBERT D.
1969 *Historical linguistics and generative grammar*. Prentice-Hall, Englewood Cliffs.

KNIFFEN, FRED
1965 Folk housing: key to diffusion. *Annals of the Association of American Geographers* 55(4):549–577.

KUHN, THOMAS S.
1970 The structure of scientific revolutions. *International Encyclopedia of Unified Sciences* 2(2). University of Chicago Press, Chicago.

LÉVI-STRAUSS, CLAUDE
1966 *The savage mind*. University of Chicago Press, Chicago.

1967 *Structural anthropology*, translated by Claire Jacobson and Brooke Grundfest Schoepf. Doubleday, Garden City.

1970a *Tristes tropiques*, translated by John Russel. Athenum, New York.

1970b *The raw and the cooked*, translated by John and Doreen Weightman. Harper and Row, New York.

LOWES, JOHN LIVINGSTON
1959 *The road to Xanadu: a study in the ways of the imagination*. Vintage Books, New York.

MASLOW, ABRAHAM H.
1969 *The psychology of science: a reconnaissance*. Henry Regnery, Chicago.

MERRIAM, ALAN P.
1964 *The anthropology of music*. Northwestern University Press, Evanston.

MERTON, ROBERT K.
1967 *On theoretical sociology: five essays, old and new*. Free Press, New York.

NORBERG-SCHULZ, CHRISTIAN
1968 *Intentions in architecture*. M. I. T. Press, Cambridge.

PACE, DAVID
1975 An exercise in structural history: an analysis of the social criticisms of Claude Lévi-Strauss. *Soundings* LVIII(2):182–199.

PANOFSKY, ERWIN
1957 *Gothic architecture and scholasticism*. World, New York.

PAREDES, AMÉRICO and RICHARD BAUMAN (Editors)
1971 *Toward new perspectives in folklore*, special issue of *Journal of American Folklore* 84.

PIAGET, JEAN
1970 *Structuralism*, translated by Chaninah Maschler. Basic Books, New York.

PIRSIG, ROBERT M.
1975 *Zen and the art of motorcycle maintenance*. Bantam Books, New York.

ROSSI, INO
1973 The unconscious in the anthropology of Lévi-Strauss. *American Anthropologist* 75(1)20–48.

SARTRE, JEAN-PAUL
1958 *Being and nothingness: an essay on phenomenological ontology*, translated by Hazel E. Barnes. Methuen, London.
1963 *Search for a method*, translated by Hazel E. Barnes. Vintage Books, New York.
SEARLE, JOHN R.
1969 *Speech acts: an essay in the philosophy of language*. Cambridge University Press, Cambridge.
STENT, GUNTHER S.
1975 Limits to the scientific understanding of man. *Science* 187(4181):1052–1057.
THOMAS, CHARLES
1960 Archaeology and folk-life studies. *Gwerin* III(1):7–17.
THOMPSON, STITH
1964 The challenge of folklore. *Publications of the Modern Language Association* LXXIX(4): 357–365.
VANSINA, JAN
1965 *Oral tradition: a study in historical methodology*, translated by H. M. Wright. Aldine, Chicago.
WILLIAMS, RAYMOND
1973 *The country and the city*. Oxford University Press, New York.
WINCH, PETER
1973 *The idea of a social science and its relation to philosophy*. Routledge and Kegan Paul, London.
YEATS, WILLIAM BUTLER
1966 *A vision*. Collier, New York.
1968 *Essays and introductions*. Collier, New York.

In Praise of Archaeology: Le Projet du Garbage

William L. Rathje

This paper is dedicated to the University of Arizona Garbage Project's official honorary mascot, Sesame Street's Oscar the Grouch. In fact, Le Projet du Garbage is based on the premise that Oscar, whose home is a trash can, knows more about the American Dream than he is telling.

Neither the considerable problems nor the products directly useful to traditional archaeologists in garbage analysis are considered in detail here. These are, or will be, available elsewhere. The point of this paper is simply that the Garbage Project and modern material culture studies like it are not dead ends; they are a new beginning for talents and expertise accrued from decades of analysis of ancient garbage.

SINCE MAN FIRST MET THE PEBBLE TOOL, his own creations have been his most important means of coping with his environment. Prob-lem after problem has been met with a material solution. Technological innovation has been heaped upon technological innovation until man is now completely enmeshed in a material network of his own making. To study any aspect of man's behavior anywhere is to study his position in that network.

This truism has rarely been taken seriously in the study of modern behavioral systems. The analysts and manipulators of our society are basically split between those who study what people say they do and sometimes how they actually behave in controlled environments, and those who invent, study and modify material things. Too often when a problem involving the interaction between people and objects arises, the solutions follow two separate courses: one based on inventing or modifying things without careful consideration of related behavior; the other based on attempts to describe and modify the ideas and actions of people without much thought to the nature of associated objects. The two courses join to a degree in some product development and market research endeavors of private business. Neither can be effective alone, as can be seen in the sea of urban renewal disasters awash in our cities.

An area where knowledge needs to be accrued in our society is at the point where theories of how people will act and how material culture will work give way to real events—observable interactions between people and things. Such a contribution does not seem to be forthcoming from modern social scientists who often overlook material culture, perhaps because they have too many people to talk to. It may, however, be brought forth out of a discipline which derived from an interest in the relics of the past. Archaeology, because of the historical accident that all the people it wants to study are dead, has been forced into looking at material things in the context of their relation to behavior. Archaeologists have begun to discover (see other papers in this symposium) that material culture is not merely a reflection of human behavior; material culture is a part of human behavior.

Can archaeologists, trained to study the interaction of people and their material networks in the past, contribute significantly to needed studies of our present society?

Archaeology pioneer Emil Haury likes to tell his audiences, "If you want to know what is really going on in a community, look at its garbage." The University of Arizona's Garbage Project has taken "Doc" Haury at his word to provide one example of the way archaeologists can attempt to contribute new insights to the understanding of contemporary problems. In addition to this goal, the Garbage Project, in the tradition of ethnoarchaeology, seeks to test the methods and theories of prehistorians in a familiar on-going society. To implement these goals, for the past three years Le Projet du Garbage has been analyzing quantifiable refuse collected in household units in Tucson, Arizona to describe the social correlates of modern urban resource management (Rathje 1974; Rathje and Hughes 1975).

The general response to the possibility of the Garbage Project significantly contributing to modern social studies can be summed up in an evaluation given by one large and prestigious funding foundation:

> The Foundation devotes its efforts to supporting social science research on problems in our society. I regret to inform you that the analysis of household refuse does not fall within the scope of our current funding program. We support research only.

Despite this kind of reaction, the student volunteers and staff of the Garbage Project have remained convinced that archaeology can contribute to knowledge of our society. The preliminary project study of the effect of inflation on food waste has strengthened that conviction.

The current spiraling cost of food for American consumers requires a concerted effort to evaluate practices which are wasteful of food resources at the household level. Little is known about household level food discard in America or anywhere else, although discarded food has been called the world's greatest unutilized food resource. If household food discard could be even partially salvaged, it would free food resources with the potential of saving lives abroad and dollars in rising prices for consumers at home.

Too often Americans try to solve their problems by concentrating *all* their efforts on the development of new technological innovations. Alternative approaches, however, are needed to supplement technological research. To get to the real roots of the problem of household level resource discard, the social correlates of food waste must be identified and studied in different contexts. This is not a simple task.

The limitations of traditional interview-survey techniques present problems for gathering accurate data on household level food discard behavior in the U.S. The concept of "food waste" is fraught with moral implications. Few Americans like to admit that they unnecessarily discard food, and mere participation in a study of waste behavior is sure to bias results. As a consequence, only a few food discard studies have been attempted. For example, in the late 1950's the USDA undertook some small studies of household food discard using records of weighed food discard kept by volunteer respondents (Adelson, *et al.* 1961: Adelson, *et al.* 1963). They utilized small nonrepresentative samples and the authors noted that the behavior of the respondents was changed by participation in the study. What is needed, then, is a means of estimating food discard which is *nonreactive*, which does not affect the behavior of the subjects (Webb, *et al.* 1966).

The Garbage Project has developed a new approach to the study of food discard (Harrison, *et al.* 1975). For the past two years in Tucson, Arizona, the project has been recording the quantifiable remnants of food consumption and discard in household trash from sample census tracts stratified by U.S. census and other income and ethnicity data. The advantage of analyzing household refuse is obvious. Interview data are always subject to questions concerning whether they represent what people do, what they think they do, or what they want an interviewer to think they do. In contrast, garbage is the quantifiable result of what people actually did.

Now that the problem and method are outlined, the challenge becomes, not only to analyze a meaningful current behavioral situation, but to do it in the context of further pursuing an archaeological concern which has a significant time-depth. The concept of "stress" is a common term in archaeology today and has been applied to almost every situation of relatively long-term, large-scale change. With food discard data it may be possible to test its utility on today's rapid economic and behavioral fluctuations.

Archaeological models suggest that at the level of a whole behavioral system, stress creates changes in actions by selecting from all available patterns of behavior those which initially meet new problems most effectively. On an individual level, since changes in behavior are required to adopt the successful patterns, archaeological stress models imply that variety will increase for most of the system's separable constituents while the transition is occurring. Thus, it will be proposed here that at an individual level there are two major phases in change due to stress: (1)heightened variety in individual activities during initial stress, followed in time by (2) generally decreased variety

in individual activities as stress abates or as people successfully adapt to it and begin to routinize their actions.

Perhaps the most interesting conclusion of archaeological studies of reaction to stress in the past is that, in the long run, changes in behavior which may be consciously aimed toward homeostasis, or stabilizing past patterns, often end in changes which do the reverse and create the unexpected (Flannery 1972; Gibson 1974; Lees 1974). Does the same irony of counterproductive reactions hold true over the short term—for example, during changes in individual behavior in the initial phases of stress? This question has ramifications which are relevant to the current level of food waste in America.

A simple efficiency model of today's behavior would suggest that under economic stress, people would discard less food. An alternate implication can be derived from the stress hypotheses in archaeology. Variety can be defined in this case in terms of the number of different kinds and quantities of items a family buys in a defined period. As people under the economic stress of rapidly rising prices change from "habits" which are no longer affordable to new and unfamiliar forms of purchasing behavior, variety may increase. This variety in household input is likely to create increased food discard. For example, new forms of bulk buying may lead to improper storage resulting in spoilage and bulk discard. Unfamiliar foods and recipes may produce unfamiliar results and unfamiliar discards. This suggests that a first reaction to increases in economic stress will be increased discard of food. Further, it may be suggested that as stress levels off or abates, people will be able to routinize their successful experiments or return to old patterns. As a result, variety and food discard will be diminished.

The alternate efficiency and stress expectations can be tentatively tested with garbage data. These data, in fact, can provide two independent tests: one involving beef, the other using most other foods. This distinction can be made on the basis of differential price rises associated with these foods between 1973 and 1974.

In the spring of 1973, when garbage food

waste data were first being systematically recorded, there was a highly publicized "beef-crisis." Beef was in short supply and prices seemed exorbitant. During the spring of 1974 beef was easy to obtain and prices were only slightly higher. Thus, based on the "efficiency" expectation, beef waste should be low during 1973 and perhaps higher in 1974. The archaeological stress model predicts the opposite: high beef waste during the 1973 shortage, lower waste during the 1974 glut.

Most other food prices show the direct inverse of beef prices, with a dramatic increase between spring 1973 and spring 1974. Thus, in relation to these commodities the expectations would be exactly the opposite. An efficiency model would expect higher waste in 1973, a stress model higher waste in 1974.

To evaluate these propositions, food input and waste data were recorded from the refuse of 226 households collected from 18 census tracts largely during February through June in 1973 and 392 households collected from 19 census tracts from February through June in 1974. Refuse from randomly selected households within sample census tracts was picked up by Tucson Sanitation Division Foremen and labeled *only* by tract to protect anonymity. Analysis was conducted at the Sanitation Division Maintenance Yard by student volunteers under the supervision of a field director. Food input data were derived from packaging and therefore did not include items like some fresh vegetables which come in unmarked wrappers. Food discard was defined as food remains that would have once been edible and is recorded by weight. No bone, separable fat, eggshells, peels, skins (except potato peels), rinds, tops, etc. are included in the category (Harrison, *et al.* 1974, 1975).

Garbage disposals, meals eaten away from home, feeding of leftover food to household pets, fireplaces, compost piles and recycling of containers, all introduce biases into the data acquired from the trash can. However, these biases all operate in one direction—they decrease the amount of refuse. Thus, garbage data can confidently be interpreted as representing *minimum* levels of household food utilization and waste. On this basis, population segments can be compared and changes over time observed.

Food discard was classified into two categories: *straight waste* is a significant quantity of an item (for example, a whole uncooked steak, half a loaf of bread, half a can of fruit); hard-to-save *plate scrapings* represent edible food in quantities of less than one ounce or unidentifiable remains of cooked dishes. Assuming that straight waste is easier to minimize than are plate scrapings, a test of the alternate models can be made in terms of rates of straight waste. The archaeology stress model, for example, expects that high waste should correlate with initial* attempts to react to rising prices; low waste should correlate, generally, with stable or decreasing prices; that there will be higher straight waste of beef in 1973 than in 1974; lower straight waste of other foods in 1973 than in 1974.

The Division of Economic and Business Research at the University of Arizona reports that in Tucson the cost of putting food on the table was, on the average, 10% higher in the spring of 1974 than in the spring of 1973. Garbage Project data for the same time periods indicate that although total food discard remained fairly constant at around 9% of food input, the percentage of food discard as plate scrapings decreased as the percentage of discard in the form of straight waste climbed from 55% of food discard in 1973 to over 60% in 1974. In some census tracts straight waste jumped from around 50% of food discard to over 80%.

It has been assumed here that straight waste may be more easily avoidable through conscious effort than is the type of food discard classified as plate scrapings. If this assumption is correct, the trend toward increasing straight waste as a proportion of total food discard in Garbage Project sample households represents a trend toward greater inefficiency in utilization of food resources, even during a period of increasing food prices and economic stress.

Waste levels of most foods follow this trend. For example, although fruit and vegetable prices were on an average of 18½% higher in the

* The analysis of long-term trends in food waste will have to await more time depth in garbage analysis.

spring of 1974 than in the spring of 1973, straight waste of fruits and vegetables did not decrease; in fact, straight waste actually increased from 16½% of household input of fruits and vegetables to 18½% of household input. The overall household input of fresh fruits and vegetables decreased by 19% between the spring of 1973 and the spring of 1974. Nevertheless, the cost of fresh fruit and vegetable straight waste, based on extrapolating from Garbage Project households to Tucson's 110,000 households, was probably $73,000 higher in the spring of 1974 over the spring of 1973.

The costs and straight waste of beef show almost the opposite trend of other foods. On the average, beef prices were up only 5% in the spring of 1974 over prices in the spring of 1973. In fact, during the month of April 1974, beef prices were 3% lower than beef prices a year earlier and in May they were almost identical. As a result, it is somewhat surprising that in 1973 weighed beef waste in sample households was 9% of beef input; in 1974 it was only 3%. The waste of beef was, therefore, almost three times higher in sampled households in 1973, during the shortage, than in 1974 during a time of a more plentiful beef supply. Using actual quantities of wasted beef and extrapolating from our sample households to Tucson, $762,000 less beef was probably wasted in the spring of 1973 than in the spring of 1974.

Thus, on the basis of Garbage Project data, straight waste seems to be, at least in the *short run*, correlated with the direction of price changes. It may be provisionally concluded that as prices go up for specific commodities, straight waste for those commodities goes up; and as prices level off, waste levels off or decreases.

As neat as this conclusion seems, in any single-dimension study there are many muddling factors. For example, the decrease in beef waste and an overall decrease in total food intake more than compensated financially for the increases in the straight waste of other items. As a result, reactions to stress in food cost culminated in a decrease of more than $500,000 in the cost of straight waste in the spring of 1974 over the spring of 1973. The question of the multivariate relation of beef and other food prices and the cost of waste to inflation still remains

open; however, many implications and further questions can be drawn from the preliminary Garbage Project results which tend to support archaeological stress models.

Using 1970 U.S. census and other data, social correlates can be related to food waste at the census tract level. Straight waste proved highest, between 70% and 85% of food waste among census tracts with no households, or under 20% of the households, below the poverty level. Straight waste was much lower, between 50% and 70% of food discard in census tracts where over 20% of the households were below the poverty level. The 1973–1974 increase in straight food waste was less dramatic in the census tracts with many poor households, and, in fact, in some of these tracts straight waste decreased. One implication of this, from an archaeological standpoint, is that for the low income census tracts, economic stress is nothing new and that few new purchasing and preparation endeavors result from increases in this type of stress.

This leads to another important point. For most census tracts, total evidence of household input of food is down in 1974 from 1973 levels. However, there were no significant changes in input patterns for census tracts with no poor households. But there were changes for households in census tracts where more than 20% of the households are below the poverty level. Their input of high protein foods decreased dramatically (meat, fish, poultry, eggs, cheese, and nuts), in some tracts by over 30%. Again the implication is that poorer neighborhoods, where economic stress has been a constant factor, can do little to adjust to increases, except to cut down on expensive foods, like meat, fish or poultry.

As in other archaeological studies there are always a few surprises. One was provided by a cluster of census tracts in which 20% to 40% of the households are below the poverty level and over 65% of the residents are Mexican-Americans. Food input remained at 1973 levels and straight waste decreased from 75% to 56% of all food waste. This same census tract cluster also exhibited a larger input of total food per household than any other population segment, a finding which is not surprising because of a relatively large household size in this subgroup. Thus the population segment which is apparently becoming more efficient in terms of waste behavior is also managing a proportionally large share of the food resources. The specific implications here are unclear, except to identify this as an important group to study further. Through this kind of analysis it might be possible to identify behaviors, and their sociocultural correlates, which result in more or less efficiency of food utilization at the household level; such information would be valuable for policy and program formulation and for a public faced with spiraling prices.

Finally, just as a sidelight, a further correlate to stress can be mentioned. There was only one product whose consumption dramatically increased between 1973 and 1974. Alcoholic beverages in 1974 made up between 15% and 25%, by volume, of all the food and beverages consumed in sample households. It is interesting to note that "efficient" tract clusters seem to imbibe the most beer at home.

Although the above data and inferences are oversimplified and highly speculative, they lay the groundwork for significant hypotheses which need rigorous testing, evaluation, and expansion in the future. This contribution is based on the fact that the Garbage Project has succeeded, in a very preliminary form, in producing the *only* quantifiable data available on some of the social correlates of food waste (Harrison, *et al.* 1974), and the relation of food waste to economic stress. However, for current problems a project's success cannot just be measured by its proposed results, but has to be measured also by the interest shown in the results by responsible social scientists and governmental planners and by the distribution of the results to the people who can learn about their behavior from them.

In the past year, the Garbage Project has received some interest from scholars and considerable publicity from the press, but much of that coverage was based on viewing garbage analysis as an academic "freak of the week" exhibit. This image is an important asset for the project to draw attention to its real contributions, and recently these contributions have been taken more seriously. On January 23,

1975, the Garbage Project reached millions of American households as the subject of a report on the NBC NIGHTLY NEWS. The project has also provided the data for consumer education articles and notes in high-circulation magazines like *Harper's* and *McCall's* and in more specialized publications like *Consumerisms*. Project results were even the subject of posters printed by the Stop and Shop grocery store chain. Finally, the Garbage Project staff is scheduled in the future to testify before Senator McGovern's Senate Select Committee on Nutrition and Human Needs.

The goal of this paper is not to demand that all archaeologists attempt to be relevant or concerned with studying the relation between modern material culture and behavior. Its only aim is to attempt to show what archaeologists can potentially extract from modern material culture studies.

First, modern material culture studies in ongoing societies can be used to test archaeological theories and methods. Even though materials change, law-like propositions and most other archaeological hypotheses should be as testable today as in the past; the same should be true of archaeological mehods in sampling and analysis.

Second, modern material culture studies can provide unique new perspectives into the nature of our own society which can make the techniques and theories of archaeology immediately useful.

For over a century archaeologists have been pushing back the frontiers of time-depth in the relation between behavior and material culture. In the past few years, early man specialists have stretched this interaction back to two million B.P. while historic archaeology and ethnoarchaeology have made contributions to the other end of the time frame. Now it is possible to utilize an archaeological perspective to study the present as it unfolds, thus defining archaeology as a discipline studying the relation between people and their possessions at all times and in all places.

The procurement, use or consumption, and discard of material things is as much a part of human behavior as speech. Through the study of these activities and their remnants, ar-

41

chaeologists can relate us to our ancestors in the past and bridge the gap from the first tool-makers to our own garbage cans.

ACKNOWLEDGEMENTS

Without the encouragement and the resourcefulness of A. Richard Kassander (University of Arizona Vice President for Research), Raymond H. Thompson (Head, Department of Anthropology, University of Arizona), and Herman K. Bleibtreu (Dean of Liberal Arts, University of Arizona), this project could not have been attempted. Tom Price, Director of Operations (City of Tucson), was the initial ingredient in the successful cooperation between the University of Arizona and the City of Tucson; Sonny Valencia, Director of Sanitation, and his staff and workmen have made the project work. The unflinching dedication of student garbage guerillas, who slogged their way through kitty litter and dinner slops has sustained the project through many dark hours. This investigation was supported by Biomedical Sciences Support Grant RR 07002 from the General Research Branch, Division of Research Resources, Bureau of Health Manpower Education, National Institutes of Health. Work is continuing through Grant AEN716371 from the RANN (Research Applied to National Needs) Division of NSF, Program for Advanced Environmental Research and Technology, and through grants from SCA SERVICES, INC., CHEVRON OIL, GENERAL MILLS, ALCOA ALUMINUM, HOFFMAN–LA ROCHE, Mr. Thomas J. Watson, Jr., and the University of Arizona College of Medicine.

This paper is the product of the ideas and criticisms of Wilson Hughes (Field Director), Frederick Gorman (Assistant Director), and Gail Harrison (Project Nutritionist).

Department of Anthropology
University of Arizona

Bibliography

ADELSON, S. F., E. ASP AND I. NOBLE
  1961 Household records of foods used and discarded. *Journal of the American Dietetic Association* 39(6):578–584.

ADELSON, S. F., I. DELANEY, C. MILLER and I. NOBLE
  1963 Discard of edible food in households. *Journal of Home Economics* 55(8):633–638.

FLANNERY, K. V.
  1968 The cultural evolution of civilization. *Annual Review of Ecology and Systematics* 3:399–426.

GIBSON, M.
  1974 Violation of fallow and engineered disaster in Mesopotamian civilization. In *Irrigation's impact on society*, edited by M. Gibson and T. Downing. *Anthropological Papers*, No. 25:7–20. University of Arizona Press, Tucson.

HARRISON, G. G., W. L. RATHJE and W. W. HUGHES
  1974 Socioeconomic correlates of food consumption and waste behavior: the garbage project. Paper presented at 1974 meeting of the American Public Health Association, New Orleans.
  1975 Food waste behavior in an urban population. *Journal of Nutritional Education* 7(1):13–16.

LEES, S. W.
  1974 The state's use of irrigation in changing peasant society. In *Irrigation's impact on society*, edited by M. Gibson and T. Downing. *Anthropological Papers*, No. 25:123–128. University of Arizona Press, Tucson.

RATHJE, W. L.
  1974 The garbage project: a new way of looking at the problems of archaeology. *Archaeology* 27(4):236–241.

RATHJE, W. L. and W. W. HUGHES
  1975 The garbage project as a nonreactive approach: garbage in . . . garbage out? In *Perspectives on attitude assessment: surveys and their alternatives*, edited by H. W. Sinaiko and L. A. Broedling. *Manpower Research and Advisory Services, Technical Report*, No. 2:151–167. Smithsonian Institution, Washington, D.C.

WEBB, E. J., D. T. CAMPBELL, R. D. SCHWARTS and L. SECHREST
  1966 *Unobtrusive measures: nonreactive research in the social sciences*. Rand McNally, Chicago.

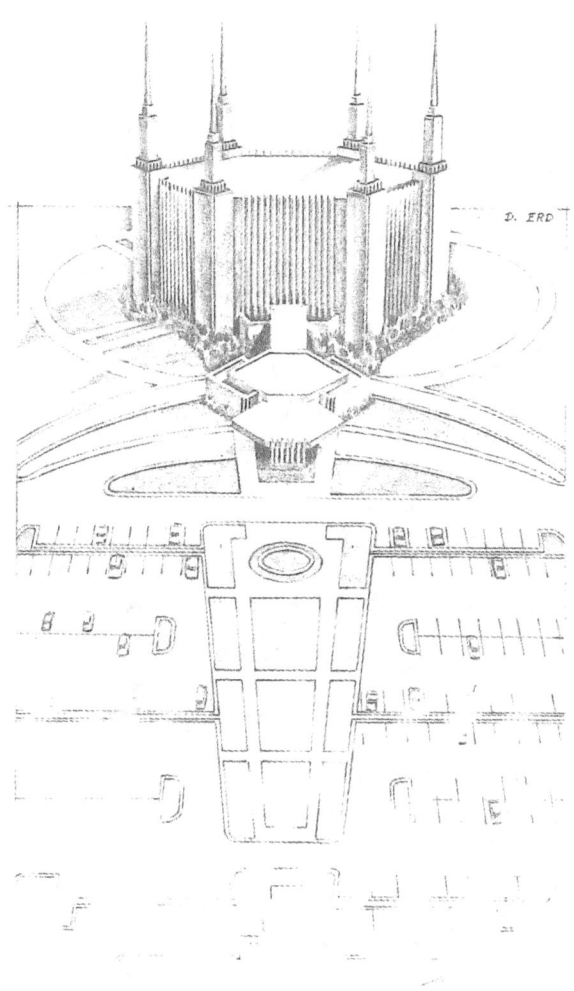

The New Mormon Temple in Washington, D.C.

Mark P. Leone

THIS ESSAY HAS ONLY ONE REAL AIM: to explain the new temple, the Washington Temple, built by the Church of Jesus Christ of Latter-day Saints (the Mormons) in Montgomery County, Maryland, just over the state line from the District of Columbia. This is a peculiar and startling building seen by tens of millions of Americans yearly and built by a church ever more prominent on the American scene. The prominence of the Mormon building and nothing else prompts this article.

I want to use a simple structural analysis to show how the pieces of the temple fit together and thus make sense. And while using a structural analysis, I would also like to call this effort a piece of historical archaeology: historical because the Mormons are literate, and archaeology because it attempts to treat a piece of material culture in its whole social context. Insofar as

the essay is these things it could also be called art history or architectural analysis or plain ethnography, but I am interested in calling it archaeology because it allows me to highlight the role of form—built, three dimensional form—in human behavior.

Every important newspaper on the East coast has written pieces on the new temple. For the most part, these occurred in the fall of 1974 but in the Washington area attention has focussed on the rising bulk of the new building towering over the Beltway for several years. The building is immense, is astonishingly visible, and attention has, not by accident, been commensurate with its growing size and visibility. While attention has been high, understanding has been low and architectural reviews have treated it as they would a new arts center, a new hotel—a reference to the involvement of the Marriott hotel family (Mormons) in the enterprise, or the most recent architectural excresence to be parodied in the service of liberal and chic causes by would-be equivalents of Tom Wolfe. There is no doubt that the temple is a fertile topic and was meant to attract attention. There is no doubt either that it does not follow many of the canons of modern architecture. There is even less doubt that what it is meant to say by its builders is heard dimly if at all by its audience, insofar as that audience consists of non-Mormons. It would be nice, to say nothing of comfortable, to say that the Mormons built the temple and started a dialogue with an eastern population, and then for us to follow the dialogue. Well, they did start one to be sure, but much of the opening rejoinder from the other side was uncomprehending abuse. But beyond that, the dialogue is peculiar because the Mormons will wave but not talk; signal, but not speak; and stun the eye but not the ear. Tourists went through the temple without guides and asked few questions of people who could give only indirect answers about temple uses which must, by oath, remain secret. For its side, attentive America usually sees the building in small intimate units as the family car goes by on a highway completely unaccompanied by identifying signs. As a result of all this, the temple has begun a conversation with its viewers, Mormon and non-Mormon, which is like that between two deaf mutes over an elephant. They both know the object is there but can not talk about what it means for each other. Neither can even be sure that the other knows the elephant is really white.

Why all the muteness? I think the answer to that lies in the nature of Mormonism, and it is obviously that nature which is both more important than the temple and is reflected in it. Mormonism, a highly public missionizing religion, is hardly silent, nonetheless in key and central ways it is silent. Above all else, it is its capacity for silence, for not integrating all its areas in public, for guarding its private worlds, for letting gestures stand uninterpreted, and for letting resultant ambiguities stand unaltered, which is its key and central way of thinking.

Once this way of thinking is understood, the meaning and muteness of the temple will be clear. The method for describing this pattern of thought involves examining what Deetz and Glassie in this volume call cognitive patterns; what Erwin Panofsky refers to as symbolical values (1955:31); and it involves what most of us know directly from Lévi-Strauss as structure. Further this is what is meant by archaeologists as style. In addition to using structure or style to understand this building, I also want to use the actual patterns of the material the temple is built of to see how it guides people's behavior and, more effectively than words, communicates the essence of Mormonism. That neither visitor nor Mormon may articulate the temple's messages is beside the point; they are there just as is the light that carries the whiteness of the elephant to the eyes of the deaf mute.

I want to preface this analysis by citing its predecessors. In a short and intriguing essay which he recently published, James Deetz (1974) talks about some of the key differences that characterize the material culture of colonial New England. His key distinction is between an early New England tradition which was essentially medieval and a later one "showing the impact of the Renaissance in the form of the Georgian tradition" (Deetz 1974:22). Using material culture, Deetz differentiated between the Middle Ages in New England and the Renaissance showing the first to be a mixture of all parts with each embedded in the other, and the second to be characterized by bilateral symmetry and the isolation of individual parts. Deetz's characterization of the medieval in New England is particular and inductive. His characterization of the Renaissance is more sweeping and structural, and illustrates better what he and Glassie mean by a cognitive pattern. It is his insight into the Renaissance which illustrates how a vast amount of material can be organized to illustrate a key pattern of thought which in turn is found in many facets of a whole culture.

This is the kind of analysis that some art historians, some architectural historians and some cultural historians have been doing for some time. It is not psychologising, but it is rather impressionistic. It is quite empirical, although as with structuralism as a whole, difficult to disprove and consequently difficult to test. Its popularity demonstrates its utility insofar as popularity demonstrates strength. I personally think that neither Glassie nor Deetz hace done much more than an impressionistic job at this type of analysis and, in not consulting the sources they might have, have missed reaching a level of generality on the Middle Ages that they did hit for the Renaissance. Certainly a key figure in establishing the critical differences between the Middle Ages and the Renaissance is Erwin Panofsky, who in dealing with form, is more precise, perceptive and general. In characterizing medieval form, Deetz talks of a "medieval assymetrical relationship between individuals and their material culture . . . the food was not consumed from individual pieces (dishes); communal containers seemed to be the rule." And, "when one walks into a pre-Georgian medieval-derived house, one walks into the whole seething range of activities from childbearing to cooking, homecraft and sleeping, all happening in one hall" (Deetz 1974:23–24). Compare this undeniably accurate description with Panofsky who, taking all of the above and all medieval art in general says, "Those who like to interpret historical facts symbolically [Deetz and Glassie using Lévi-Strauss would say cognitively] may recognize in [Renaissance art] . . . a specifically 'modern' conception of the world which permits the subject to assert itself against the object as something independent and equal; whereas classical antiquity did not as yet permit the explicit formulation of this contrast; and whereas the Middle Ages believed the subject as well as the object to be submerged in a higher unity" (Panofsky 1955:99). What Deetz saw for medieval style was the individual submerged in the mass, but what he did not see was that functions were completely absorbed in each other. The Renaissance in creating bilateral symmetry did indeed create the individual—and separate dining plates as well as Deetz's famous separate chamber pots—but it also isolated functions so that as Deetz says, "When one walks into the door of a Georgian house, one sees doors. And when one walks through those doors, one is very likely to see even more doors before getting to the final activity that is going on" (Deetz 1974:24).

So to clarify, but not to disagree with Deetz, the cognitive pattern or style of the Middle Ages

is, "repetition of form (rhyme as opposed to meter!) and verticalism," (Panofsky 1955:188) while that of the Renaissance is bilateral symmetry. The Middle Ages separates neither individual, nor function, nor time; the Renaissance invented the individual, distinguished the parts of society, and discovered history. In the Renaissance discovery of perspective, which is a spatial as well as a temporal concept as Panofsky has pointed out (1955:51) and as John Rowe has reported to anthropologists (1965:1–20), there is a segmented view of the world which resides in the relationship of man to man, man to space, and man to time. Not only were these distinctions not available to or discovered by the Middle Ages, they, in addition, resulted in the Renaissance theory of proportions which was used by Renaissance artists and, which, when imposed on form, resulted in the appearance of organically real images. The "real" was created through the use of an illusion. The picture was the illusion, the technique used to create the illusion was perspective, and the structure or style of the illusion was a particular form of symmetry: bilateral, in which each side exhibits a regular repeated pattern of the component parts.

It was with perspective that the individual could be isolated from the group or mass; that time could be segmented giving rise to one of its units, history; and space divided with some "accuracy." All this is what bilateral symmetry means. It is what is inherent in style or structure, and what is revealed by a study of the effects of such a "cognitive pattern" on a culture.

The value of this kind of structural, iconological or stylistic analysis resides in the broad applicability of the insight to masses of data from the era and culture. It obviously—linking Panofsky's high art and Deetz plebian artifacts—enfolds all material form within a society, but additionally can profitably be applied to forms like music, dance, theatre, forms of social organization, and rather logically, myth. As archaeologists, we are clearly concerned with material culture and as such the light that Deetz and Glassie are focussing on the discipline with their work highlights the problem we have traditionally known as style. In linking up

45

with Lévi-Strauss both Deetz and Glassie have, rather inadvertently, both identified what style is and shown us how to analyse it. Even though the job is impressionistic and by Lévi-Strauss' canons of detailed work, undone, the benefits to be drawn are intriguing, and since this essay too deals with a literate group, to say nothing of a living one, it is useful to attempt just such an effort.

THE CHURCH OF JESUS CHRIST OF LATTER-DAY SAINTS has built eighteen temples from Switzerland to San Paulo, and Hawaii to New Zealand. For a Mormon the temple is as close to the other-worldly as he can come on earth. The temple is God's residence rather more than the local chapel where he does most of his worshipping and all of his congregational meeting. A Mormon visits a temple once a year as a kind of norm, but may go everyday, or several times a year. He may also go much less frequently than once a year. But he cannot be a good Mormon and avoid the temple.

Mormons go through a series of rites in the temple which guarantee them and their relatives, living and dead, the rewards the church promises in the next life. The ceremonies are long and complex, take the nature of initiation rites centering on the individual and his family, and do not center on the group or congregation. They are the most sacred and meaningful acts a Mormon can perform.

After its dedication, a temple is permanently closed to all non-Mormons and any Mormon who has not paid a full tithe or has broken the Word of Wisdom, which forbids smoking, and alcoholic as well as caffeinated drinks. There are other more general requirements about quality of faith and so on. In addition, the temple rites are secret; Mormons generally do not discuss them outside the temple itself. All this elevates the temple experience to one that is unique and highly unusual and makes the temple a place of total security, for in it the faithful Mormon is in contact with both his deceased relatives and his own future. Time stands still in this building; or better, it is compressed. Time is overcome.

The series of ceremonies in the temple which insure spiritual well-being fall into three categories: (1) baptism, (2) a series of ritual dramas unfolding the spiritual history of man and during which participants receive endowments which are gifts from the Holy Ghost concerning admission to and behavior in the most exalted sphere of the next life, and (3) sealing, during which living and dead relatives are joined to each other for all eternity.

These ceremonies, which are available to any Mormon who meets the requirements for entering the temple, are participated in by family units and to bring families there often, a whole group of ward members (associates from a parish) will go through the temple the same day, although not necessarily through any or all of the ceremonies together. A temple like the new one in Washington will have a complex schedule, and for all the Mormons it serves on the East coast, eastern Canada, and in the Caribbean, it will set aside several times during the year when specific wards should plan to send members. Since it takes several hours to go through all the temple rites and since a temple may serve a population of a hundred thousand, these buildings often operate at night as well as during the day.

Every temple has a president, a vast staff which is made up of local volunteers who act as guides, instructors and workers in the temple performances. A temple like the one in Washington has a cafeteria for workers, a laundry for the special garments required during the rites, and a whole support staff to maintain self-sufficiency while operating.

The design and layout of the new temple are remarkable. It rises well above the usual or conventional in church architecture and provides one of the keys to a literal as well as a symbolic understanding of the nature of the temple rites. As opposed to the expectation of most laymen, the temple is not one vast open space for group worship like a cathedral. Rather it is composed of seven floors, six of which are broken up into many small ceremonial chambers. The top floor, the seventh, is a single hall called the Solemn Assembly Room; it is essentially an auditorium and is almost never used. It does not figure in the temple rites and most Mormons never visit it. Not all floors in the Washington

Temple are designed the same way but several of the ceremonially most important are divided into six pie-shaped rooms and are linked by a corridor running around them along the wall of the building. The temple's basic ground plan is hexagonal and this plan is followed on some inside floors so that six more-or-less triangular rooms efficiently divide the space on a floor. These rooms do not seem to lead into each other, but let into the circumferential corridor which ties them all together.

The many floors are linked together by two monumental staircases at either end of the building; these ascend through the two main towers at each extreme point of the temple. Elevators also do the same job and next to each on the appropriate floor is a hexagonal map of the floor you are on showing the numbered ceremonial rooms with lights behind so the viewer can tell at a glance which are occupied by ongoing rites. One gets the impression when going through the temple of a vast assemblage of rooms arranged in relation to each other in a way which is not at all readily apparent. I think the best way to convey the effect is to say that during the public tours in the fall of 1974 maybe a hundred people were admitted as a group every twenty to thirty minutes, which meant that hundreds of people were roaming through the building at their own pace at any one time. Yet half-way through this self-guided tour it was difficult to see another person. The building is so large and contains so many rooms it merely absorbs people. It was quite possible to be alone, removed and peacefully at ease without seeing or being seen by another person. These are useful, if personal observations, because they reflect the highly individual, and private nature of the experience Mormons have in this building. It is very much tailored to the self and the idiosyncratic.

The individual goes through the temple for himself and is often accompanied by relatives—husband, wife and children. Socially it is a family experience in a very profound sense because the family ties are given eternal permanence in the temple, but spiritually and psychologically Mormons talk about the experience in deeply personal terms; it has its deepest

impact on the individual. Its purpose is not to create group unity or communitas. The temple and its rites are about order; they create a continuous line of relatives stretching back through the otherwise personally meaningless epochs of history and do this through vicarious baptism for dead kinsmen, and through endowments and sealings projecting the family forward to infinity. The temple guarantees order in history and reduces the future to a function of acts performed now. Since all the temple rites use kinship as the basis for organization, every participant is an ego and builds his world, to be sure a magical vision of one, accordingly. An individual does this only once for himself; all other times he assumes the ego of a relative or even someone else's relative.

Mormons express this interplay between the individual and the group—be it family or church—by using the image of a beehive. Joseph Smith initiated this symbolism, which reached its culmination during the church's Utah period in the nineteenth century. Deseret, the name for the Saintly kingdom, meant honey bee in "Reformed Egyptian," according to the Prophet. The beehive with the motto "Industry" became the visual image of the Territory of Utah and later of the state. Brigham Young built his famous Beehive House, his official residence with a big, carved beehive on the top of it. The beehive expressed the relationship of the individual to the ordered whole: the individual can realize himself only through his place in the whole. The symbolism is very old in this church, is conscious and recognized by all members, and has been elaborated at one time or another before all Mormons. Consequently it is neither an accident nor a particularly unconscious action that the new Washington Temple is hexagonal, the basic geometric pattern inside a beehive. Temples, like beehives, build and demonstrate order, and the individual who goes through one is shown order and is empowered to create the very order he witnesses. The beehive imagery allows us to see the relationship between the individual and the whole in Mormonism, a relationship far more emphatic, far more latent with atomism, and sponsoring far more independence and idiosyncracy than we usually see in Christian churches. Although this will be clearer later, I have raised the imagery here to stress the point that the temple insures order but does so for ego as opposed to the group.

The order and certainty of the beehive are both emphasized and partially created by the temple's location. To get to it one must use the Beltway and go through the traffic of one of the country's biggest, busiest, most depersonalizing and frightening highways. One Mormon, no doubt speaking for many others, has commented on the "contrast between Washington traffic and the peace of the temple." It is "like going to Heaven and coming back again." The order and certainty of the temple are highlighted by the experience on the highway where uncertainty, tension, the immediacy of possible disorder, and the nearly total lack of contact with, and concern for, fellow human beings are ali bred. Consequently the temple is even more meaningful because it represents guaranteed surcease and because the Mormon can see a truth which frees him from the mad world he has just driven through and which must, in sending him back to that same world, leave him changed and stronger. It does this by showing the Mormon his individual place within life and beyond it, and does so by immersing him in disorder as he approaches the building and by immersing him in order once he is in it.

So far this paper has been a description of the temple and its purpose for Mormons. The only thread that should come through to this point is that the temple is not a usual church building. Part of its unusualness arises from (1) its stress on the individual and his family, rather than the congregation and (2) the individual's relationship to order. How is order created?

The Mormon lives successfully both in the world of outside chaos and the world of order within the church. We can assume he does so because, among other reasons, his temple experience shows and instructs him how to. Mormon successes in business, government, management, and finance are too well celebrated to need relating here. Mormons and Mormonism handle the real world very well on their own terms. Since the temple rites partake of heaven ("eternal things"), the transcenden-

tal and unempirical are the highest things a living Mormon can experience. This is puzzling in the face of Mormon worldly success. Many modern Christians, it can be argued, are quite successful in the world and believe in transubstantiation, the efficacy of prayer and the reality of magic. Yet what the Mormon experiences in the temple is more personal, coherent, more enveloping and, I would suggest, requires a bigger leap of faith if only because it is so new and untraditional, so ungrounded in popular acceptance, and so all-encompassing. The temple rites are extravagantly systematic in what they encompass of a man's life. They are supposed to effect one's life deeply, and rather obviously do just that judging from what participants say. These are unlike most Christian rituals, and for that reason are more difficult to compartmentalize out of existence. So the question is: How can Mormons negotiate being Mormon and being in the world simultaneously. And the answer is: Success comes not despite the peculiarity of the messages received in the temple, but because of them. And to go one step further, the messages about the next life obviously deal with something unempirical, but the way those messages are delivered is very empirical and in fact forms the basis for what a Mormon takes from the temple in order to deal successfully with daily life. There is one general piece of information a Mormon takes from the temple. This is the knowledge of his place as a specific individual in the endless family.

Recall the silence of the temple (Mormons cannot talk about it outside even with each other, and must remain silent during the ceremonies) and the emphasis on meditation and reflection. Discussion in the temple is usually with a spouse or son or daughter. Individuals, knowing they are closer to God here, sometimes have visions and revelations, something Mormons are entitled to concerning themselves and their families. Ceremonies are small and culminate in securing one's own or a relative's place in the family for the next life. The whole takes place in the multitudinous vastness of this very broken up and isolating building. There is no emphasis on what is going on for anyone else, anywhere else and, indeed, there is no real way to find out. The individual is alone (but never lonely) with his family and his thoughts. On these last he is encouraged to spend time, to resolve issues and questions of deep concern so that he can receive illumination. There is no discussion and certainly no checking on either the questions or the answers taken away from the ceremonies. Answers to personal questions derived from inspiration could no more be questioned than a man's right to pray for them. All this is sponsored in the temple, and coincides with much other Mormon speculating and theologizing at a personal level in Sunday Schools and Sacrament Meetings (Leone 1974). It is interesting here because of the high level of idiosyncratic interpretation guaranteed to Mormons on spiritual matters. This level of personal interpretation is prefaced in the ambiguity of the temple's identity as one approaches it, the silence while one is in it, the isolation with one's thoughts, the aim of the ceremonies to secure one's past and future, and the highly fragmenting and atomizing nature of the building itself. Mormons usually expect to have a deeply personal, spiritual and moving experience in the temple.

I would not argue that what Mormons do in establishing personalized meanings is different in kind from what Americans do in general, but it is certainly different in degree. The difference can be summed up architecturally when the profile of the six-spired temple is compared against the stereotype of American churches: the single spired unit. The unity, comprehensiveness, and singleness symbolized by the one tower on the standard American Protestant church is so obviously in contrast to the complex of pinnacles on the temple that the meaning of this most public of Mormon images is deliberately highlighted. The towers do have explicit iconographic significance insofar as they represent the two orders of the Mormon priesthood, each of which has three internal subdivisions. This of course matches not only the six towers, but their grouping in two sets, with one set higher than the other thus matching the relative importance of the two orders. Each set of three is also ordered in height thus also matching the grades within the two priesthood orders. Aside from marking the definite maleness of the building, the towers are a clue

to the internal compartmentalization of the building. They mark not a single unit, but a plurality of them. This does not mean by inference that Mormons have an ununified or incompletely synthesized theology, but it does mean that their method for arriving at unity is far more diversified than standard Protestant Christianity, and indeed since the six towers stand for all Mormon men (who are simultaneously all priests) *vs.* the single Protestant tower which symbolizes unity of faith as defined by its theologians, what we do have in these pinnacles is an index to the fact that theology is in the hands of all adults and that faith is defined by all Mormons. Thus the many towers indicate huge potential diversity of meaning within the church as well as the individuality necessary to bring that about.

Mormons have invented a very diffuse system in which each believer takes the Reformation injunction that every man be his own priest and moves a further step, namely, that he be his own theologian as well. This is a complex theme that can not be developed here except to say that such a system of idiosyncratic meanings needs careful sponsorship and equally careful control. Its sponsorship comes in the many settings for and prescriptions to discuss the meaning of the faith in terms of everyday problems. It comes in the way ego must be fitted into the whole in the temple. Personal construction of meaning can proliferate freely only if, in addition to its being encouraged, it is not seen as being in conflict either with what other Mormons believe or with other segments of itself.

The particularity of the temple and its many isolated chambers preface, in an architectural sense, and help guarantee, in a deterministic sense, the particularity of beliefs which can be found from Mormon to Mormon. The categories or compartments which exist in any one Mormon's world view and in which he holds incompatible ideas apart from each other are all liscensed here. Incompatible ideas stem from any system which involves secret oaths, private knowledge, ongoing revelations and visions from the beyond. It stems from believing in Biblical literalism and ongoing revelation; from holding alleged racial attitudes and backing civil rights for all; from opposition to evolutionary biology and believing in the evolution of knowledge; from sponsoring sexual prudery while frankly enjoying sex in private. This amounts to saying that Mormons like all believers must juggle discrepancies and contradictions, but, unlike most other Christians, they must do it individual by individual without professional thinkers to invent syntheses from them.

The highly compartmentalized and much commented on mode of thought that results from this is as much reflected in the temple as it is sponsored by the way the rituals and apparatus of the temple operate. The structural, cognitive or stylistic principle behind all this is: close but mutually exclusive categories. As the medieval was form piled on form vertically, and the Renaissance was bilateral symmetry, so the Mormon is real but unseen contradiction. Any culture's mode of thought obviously must consist of categories and oppositions, but it is how they are combined that gives rise to the differences between groups. And beyond that, for many cultures, categories do touch and overlap as was the case in the Middle Ages (recall Deetz's medieval house) and may even be considered well-integrated as was the case with the Renaissance. (The well-known idea of the Renaissance man expressed just such integration.) Such integration either does not exist for Mormons or, if it does, happens in a rather unusual way.

Not only do Mormons live in a world of categories, but those categories are of a distinct type. Not to be too esoteric or too removed about it, consider the following quote.

Most Americans believe that a moral issue can be contained within a category, and they often find themselves astonished or irritated by those Americans who do not. A lot of University trustees can't imagine why students who are receiving a perfectly peaceful liberal education should concern themselves with the fact some other department of the same institution happens to do research for the Department of Defense. Most Americans do not hold a Rockefeller in New York accountable for what kind of regime his family's bank helps support in South Africa. But a lot of black people and young people insist on considering everything connected. Because Brigham Young University, which is operated by the Mormon Church, happens to be one of the few places in the country where even the students believe in the sanctity of

categories, it is difficult for nearly everyone there to understand how objection to a Mormon religious belief could be translated into rudeness to the B. Y. U. basketball team. In reaffirming that priesthood orders, which every male Mormon must hold in order to participate fully in the Church, would remain closed to Negroes, the First Presidency clearly stated not only that the matter was wholly within the category of religion but also that in the civil category the Church specifically teaches that all of God's children should have equal constitutional rights. Furthermore, the University's president has pointed out, the Church has nothing to do with arranging athletic events; and, furthermore, the coaches often say, some of the players are not even Mormons, and the athletic field would obviously not be the place to argue politics or religion even if they were. Yet B.Y.U. basketball players can hardly appear anywhere without being hooted at as racists, and Stanford University announced last fall (1970) that it would no longer meet B.Y.U. in athletic contests. Keeping the argument within its original category, Ernest L. Wilkinson, the president of B.Y.U., called Stanford's action 'flagrant religious discrimination' (Trillin 1970:120).

Mormon categories are exceptional in two ways. They are often, as with the quote, at variance with and contradictory to the categories of the surrounding, dominant society. Furthermore, they are, in a system which depends on revelation for its logic, frequently at odds with themselves. This does not make the system unique, in fact it probably accounts for its considerable strength, but it does make the position of any individual Mormon more sensitive to the cognitive adjustments the world demands than ordinary Americans have to be. After all, we as average natives in the dominant society are not forced at every turn to compare our notions to those of some superior power. Further, there are masses of clever people whose job it is to juggle for us any discrepancy into the proper shape when it appears. What we as average Americans face the Mormon must do individually. He is very good at it, is given a lot of practice, and in the temple rites is shown how to hold the world together.

What clashing categories do Mormons bring to the temple? Mormons are encouraged to bring their problems to the temple, and some do visit the temple during times of personal crisis. All do expect deeply personal and integrating experiences there. There are other expectations as well. Originally, of course, Mormons expected the millennium momentarily and to some extent they still do. The crisis of that non-event as well as of continuing persecution are also brought to the temple. So, to some extent one comes to the temple with something on one's mind. Consider then the pressures the ordinary Mormon is under in his day-to-day life, pressures no more acute than those arising from having to make sense of the world within a religion which is most public about its most spectacular differences with America (formerly polygamy, now the place of the black), and then match these against what actually happens in the sacred ceremonies.

The following is a general account of the ceremonies drawn from several sources.

> The core of the rites involve a ritual drama. The creation of the world and the 'Fall' of man in the Garden of Eden, respectively. In the 'World Room' Satan's preachers are ridiculed as they present their devilish opinions . . . (then) there is a recognition of the restoration of the 'gospel' to earth through the Prophet Joseph Smith. The culmination . . . occurs in the 'Celestial Room' ('heaven') which is entered through a sacred veil from the 'Terrestial Room.' This veil is the ultimate link, or alternately the boundary, between heaven and earth. The ritual [which is roughly three hours long] concludes with the 'sealing' ceremonies which join husbands and wives or parents and children for 'time' and for 'eternity.' The rites may be participated in for the living (oneself) or for the dead, in which case the individual serves as 'proxy' for a particular dead ancestor or friend. At appropriate stages throughout the rites the various 'degrees' of the Aaronic and Melchizedek Priesthoods are conferred upon the participants, who recite oaths under specific penalties of bodily harm that will befall the unfaithful (Dolgin 1974:536).

The ritual drama which individuals watch is played out by temple functionaries who portray Adam, Eve, Lucifer, Jehovah, Elohim, the Lord and various apostles. Elohim is God the Father, Jehovah is Christ, and Lord, another word for God the Father. In the dialogue between these heavenly persons the key ceremonial acts are set out (Whalen 1964:177–179). The dialogue between them is a set script, and is both modern and compelling. In the dialogue Adam, who represents man, listens to a typified Protestant preacher expound his views at Lucifer's urging. Adam finds the views wanting,

rejects them and describes himself as waiting for God to enlighten him truly. This is a fragment of the drama which is followed by more conversation between the protagonists who are basically God and the Devil. The audience is represented by and asked to identify with Adam, one who waits, seeks and is fulfilled. This particular part of the ritual drama enunciates the dilemma facing every Mormon: how to believe what he knows to be true while the majority of people he is surrounded by in daily life remains steadfastly indifferent, to say nothing of opposed. How to remain faithful and different?

Later in the ceremonies just before entering the final or Celestial Room the individual Mormon approaches the veil separating it from the Terrestrial Room and is actually interviewed by the Lord and shakes hands with him. The participant whispers his secret temple name into the Lord's ear and presents the various signs of the priesthoods which were bestowed during the immediately preceding rites. He then crosses the veil, joins the Lord and enters heaven in the Celestial or Glory Room. To recall a phrase used earlier from a Mormon who had been through the temple, "It's like going to Heaven, and coming back again." Mormons clearly know they have neither talked to God personally nor been in heaven, but they talk as though they have experienced something quite real, not a set of elaborate metaphors. What does the drama mean? How does it highlight ego and his place in the eternal family? And what does it do to allow a Mormon to live successfully and happily in a world so at odds with his religion?

I think the place to seek an answer is in Lévi-Strauss' analysis of myth in *The Effectiveness of Symbols* (1963:186–205).

Lévi-Strauss tells how a woman undergoing difficult childbirth was treated by a shaman who told her a myth of a gigantic struggle, a telling which eased and delivered the birth. Lévi-Strauss likens the relationship between the pregnant woman and the shaman to that between a patient and a psychoanalyst. The shaman invites the woman to be absorbed in the myth, to experience the genuinely intense but abnormal pain she is feeling, pain which the shaman tells her is part of the struggle of the supernaturals elaborated in the myth. By allowing the woman to come to terms with, and to fully experience the pain, tension and contradiction of her situation, the shaman eases the birth. By listening to the myth of violent and gargantuan struggle, a struggle which, according to the myth, is being played out in her loins right now, the woman can give free development to the conflicts and resistances inherent in her situation and can do so in a way allowing for their resolution. Lévi-Strauss suggests that all this is effective even though the role of speaker is reversed, with the therapist talking and the patient listening.

There are three elements involved in this analysis: (1) the individual who is experiencing some troublesome conflict, (2) the recitation to this involved audience of a conflict of transcendent importance which is being played out right now inside him or her, and (3) a transference relationship between listener and speaker.

Reflecting back now on the temple rites, recall that Mormons enter the temple under two simultaneous conditions. They come there expecting a deeply moving experience, one which is personal and fulfilling. Any Mormon entering the temple will also face two other problems; these being his general reason for doing temple work. He faces the problem, as does his whole church, of redeeming all those generations of mankind who lived before the "restoration of the Gospel," i.e. before the advent of Mormonism. This problem is double faceted: why was the church founded so late in time? and why were previous generations excluded from it? This is a problem about how to view the past.

The second paradox which every Mormon faces just because he is a Mormon and incidentally because he is a Christian as well, is the non-event of the promised millennium. The Prophet Joseph unambiguously promised the Second Coming before the generation to whom he was speaking passed away. Mormons are allowed very free personal rein in suggesting when Christ will return to earth and many expect to see him in their lifetime. Nonetheless Christ has not come and Joseph's generation has passed away. That problem is doubly poignant because the Second Coming would establish a bliss that would show both the triumph of

the church and an end to its persecution, the latter being something Mormons still dwell on and from time to time genuinely experience. That they may invite it unawares may indicate how essential that persecution is to maintaining millennial expectations.

The effectiveness of reciting a myth about a blissful future to a congregation disappointed in its millennial hopes has been pointed out by John Gager (1975:43–57) in an illuminating analysis of that rather obscure text, the *Book of Revelation*, St. John's Apocalypse. The telling of the myth about the millennium to a group who expects it immediately allows the group, in Lévi-Strauss' use of Freud, to experience directly and thus to resolve the conflicts between the promised coming and its non-fulfillment, and between continued persecution and unarrived bliss.

Consider then what is going on for the Mormon in the temple. He brings expectations of profound experience and sometimes specific problems to be solved. Narrated before him by supernatural personages is the whole of human history comprising the creation, fall and redemption of man. At one point there is actually verbal and physical contact with God himself and then God actually invites the purified to enter and experience heaven. Throughout the narrations people are listening to Adam, God the Father and Christ talk, not as read by a reader out of the Gospels, but by people playing the heavenly beings. And for additional emotional impact the audience overhears private, off-stage conversations between God, Christ, Peter and others making plans to redeem man based on his worthy performance. If he believes what he is hearing, the Mormon is hearing a level of reality not present even in *Revelations*.

The contradictions in the past and the future are overcome, and so consequently is time. Time is held still and all the paradoxes arising as a result of the way time does indeed pass are faced and resolved in the temple experience which is a long, fully participatory, emotionally profound recitation and enactment of the answers to life's basic questions.

I have suggested two sets of problems any Mormon faces when going through the temple: the problem of the past and future on one hand

and, on the other, specific problems which we suppose derive from experiencing the arbitrariness and incoherence of the world, especially as it conflicts with Mormonism. The degree to which this consciously presses on a Mormon must vary a great deal and it is quite possible that most Mormons enter the temple without specific awareness of any strong problem in particular. Nonetheless every Mormon is aware of the fact that he is different from all other Americans, and that those differences, while central to his religion and well being, are peculiar and often invite persecution. The Mormon then goes through an emotionally compelling ritual which narrates his basic fears, rejection by his Father, a consequently chaotic world, the tremendous power of the world's temptations, the great fear that he cannot remain steadfastly separate against them, and the horrendous punishments awaiting him outside the faith. He is treated to reunion with his dead relatives, permanent union into the next life with his closest kin; he enjoys the sight of God and enters what can only be regarded as a foretaste of eternal bliss. A whole set of the profoundest crises are faced for what they are, with their full implications for all to see.

The Mormon comes to the temple as a member of a family unit. Even if he goes through it alone, he is working for his dead relatives, and ultimately will enter the Celestial Room paired with a Mormon woman, which means that one enjoys the fullest level of heavenly bliss only in conjunction with one's family. Only through her husband can a woman enjoy this ultimate exaltation and only with a wife can a man. The unit is not bigger than the family and, although the family is in theory inclusive of all mankind, emphasis is on the nuclear family. And given the nature of kinship, ties are always calculated from ego, or the individual, which means that while the family unifies, kinship ultimately atomizes. Each person is given a secret temple name and uses it to identify himself to the god-impersonator. This level of individuality which must be seen as important in allowing a Mormon to solve his individual problems, to resolve his own paradoxes, to address what is peculiarly incoherent and arbitrary in his own life, is given free reign in the

temple. The individual has time to meditate, pray, may and often does have visions, receives personal revelations, and from what we may judge from modern Mormons and from the ecstatic experiences commonly attributed to temple work in Joseph's and Brigham's lifetimes, may enjoy other altered states of consciousness as well. I think we may assume that the union of the general and specific problems encountered in the temple helps heighten the experience a Mormon has there since he can understand the general problems via his own specifics and his own problems in terms of the solution to the general ones. Each is essential to working out the other.

The temple context is one of several where a Mormon can work out the paradoxes created by and resolved through the way he sees the world. Here he overcomes time to experience both past and future, and overcomes space to experience spirit persons dwelling in another world. By experiencing such a melting of categories into each other the Mormon can tolerate the incoherence and arbitrariness he lives with daily. His own mode of thought seems to be to hold onto incommensurable notions, notions which are all quite essential to existence. The separation, although part of living a good Mormon life, creates a tension which is resolved through the temple rites. The resolution can be only temporary since Mormons cannot change the world or their place in it. Both their place in it, a subordinate one given their status as a religious and economic minority, and the success they have made in exploiting their position, exert some pressure to maintain things as they are. Since Mormons are very American and very Mormon, and since to be Mormon is to be both suspicious of America and to be ultra-American, any Mormon may love his society and be in rebellion against it at the same time. He is perforce divided and lives in society and apart from it; he must live in and think about very close but quite exclusive categories. And if the categories are not maintained, his distinctness is eliminated and his identity along with it; also lost would be his ability to adjust to the demands of being a member of a minority, in short, his way of earning a living.

Now reflecting back on the temple we can see

that the experience connected with it keeps a man a whole individual by helping him resolve the tensions of being Mormon, which in turn allows him to continue using the same conflicting categories that come from daily life, categories which make his participation in it possible in the first place. All this categorization, the very close but exclusive categories are seen in the physical aspect of the temple: the compartments, the floors, the lockers, the lighted maps showing which of the many rooms are in use, the multitude of towers and the silence. All this planning can now be understood in terms of the general structural or cognitive principle that informs Mormonism; close but mutually exclusive categories. The temple isolates the individual, resolves that isolation, but does so only to plunge the individual back into it again when the ceremonies are over. So unlike psychotherapy and Lévi-Strauss' childbirth myth, but rather like Gager's analysis of the function of St. John's *Book of Revelation* to its first century listeners, the tension is resolved but not eliminated: the future cannot be realized but merely assured, or perhaps glimpsed.

To step back now outside the Mormon world and to reflect on the ambiguous dialogue the temple sets up with its isolated viewers, I would like to explore how the building and the way it is treated maintains the same basic structural relationship in its silent conversation with the outside world.

The new temple can be isolated by creating a series of oppositions. The Washington Temple, actually located twenty to thirty minutes from downtown Washington, can be seen against the other national religious monuments in the Washington area. It can be compared with the National Cathedral which is Episcopal, and the National Shrine which is Catholic. There are obviously many others, but comparison with these two will make the point. The Washington Temple can also be seen against the other Mormon temples, mostly against those in the Great Basin of the western United States.

When we compare the new temple with the other national religious buildings in Washington we learn that the National Cathedral was begun in the 1880s and is not going to be finished for more than another decade, that the

Catholic Shrine was begun early in this century and is still being decorated, and that, as opposed to this, the Washington Temple was begun in 1971 and completely finished in three years.

The National Cathedral is a Gothic building which has been built using only material appropriate to the style; there is no steel or reinforced concrete in it. The Catholic Shrine is a Byzantine building also employing technology which is thought to be appropriate to the style. The Mormon temple is completely modern. Stylistically it is closest to the Kennedy Center for the Performing Arts and technologically it is as modern as the Mormons could make it. It contains 16,000 tons of reinforced concrete.

The National Cathedral and Catholic Shrine were continually plagued with financial troubles. The Mormons raised at least two million dollars more among themselves than they needed to pay for the building.

The Cathedral, the Shrine, and the Temple are all tourist attractions. They are all set in parks, welcome the general public, have tours and were all consciously constructed to attract both the faithful and the curious. In short, they all use themselves as missionizing devices. But except for the six weeks when it was open to the general public before its dedication, the interior of the Mormon temple is closed to all but worthy Mormons. You can walk around it, but there is no entry.

What can be seen when the Washington Temple is compared to Utah temples? The Washington Temple is the only one east of the Mississippi, aside from two in Europe. Since most Mormon temples are in the Great Basin, they are also incidentally in deserts; succulent deserts to be sure, but semi-arid deserts nonetheless. The Washington Temple sits on a lush green Maryland hillside with no other buildings in sight—just green woodland. Utah temples are always in towns. The Washington Temple is on a hillside overlooking the Beltway, Route 495, that carries millions of cars annually past it on the way north and south around Washington. The temple is, however, isolated and is not part of any visible community; it is nonetheless the most visible thing on the beltway.

All Mormon temples are surrounded by lush

gardens; the garden around the temple in Washington is very attenuated. All Utah temples are rectangular; the Washington Temple is hexagonal. Utah temples have one or two towers that are uncrowned with any symbol. The Salt Lake Temple has six towers the highest of which is topped with an angel blowing a trumpet. The Washington Temple, consciously copying the Salt Lake Temple in this respect, has six towers, three at either end, and the highest tower has an angel blowing a trumpet on top.

So the Mormons have built a temple which quite consciously is not in a desert, not in a town, and does not have a real garden. It mirrors their major visual symbols: the beehive, the Salt Lake Temple towers, the trumpeting angel, and sits on a bluff overlooking the passing world. It is also the biggest and most expensive temple of the eighteen the Mormons have built.

All we can conclude so far is that the Washington Temple is a very unusual national church and a very unusual Mormon temple. What are the Mormons trying to accomplish with this building? Consider the millions who drive by it on the beltway. And the 800,000 people who toured it in the six weeks between early September and mid-October 1974. But consider also that for most people who will ever see it, the building must remain a mystery; they can never get in. The temple begins to look like a prominent paradox. It is astonishingly visible; it glitters and dazzles above the highway with its gold towers and white marble walls. And yet it is ultimately remote. Its style is an easily recognizable mixture of contemporary, Edward Durell Stone, art nouveau, Disney World, and a touch of Gothic. It is a workable pastiche of the architectural cliches of the late 1960s and early 1970s. In short, it is a familiar building, and a very American building. But it belongs to a group of people whom every viewer knows used to be polygamous and who are today, depending on the viewer's outlook, blatantly racist, suffering from the Negro problem, or simply honest about their racial preferences. Now neither polygamy nor exclusion of blacks is very American. And so we have added to the paradox of high visibility but no accessibility, the paradox of an easily identified American building built by a group who have been and continue to be

capable of quite un-American behavior. The temple is becoming a peculiar building. It is even more so when the passer-by realizes that he thinks of Mormonism as a small religion somewhere in the West. And then remembers that the death of God was proclaimed almost a decade ago. Yet, paradoxically here is a religion healthy enough to build a $15,000,000 building right under his very nose. These are the obvious puzzles to be read out of a non-Mormon view of the Washington Temple.

For Mormons this temple is the visible symbol of their arrival on the East coast, of their success in the center of power. All of the visibility, money, and speed in construction the temple signals are deliberate messages the Mormons want to give. They are coming to national power and prominence; they are very rich, very well-organized and disciplined. The temple, as one Mormon said, "is built to last." It is also built to correct—better to change—the national stereotype used to characterize Mormons. Not only does the temple obviously demonstrate that the church is alive, well, big, rich, and powerful, more to the point for Mormons, it says Mormons are growing, rich, and powerful in the heart of the East.

Further it says they are Christians. The question most frequently asked of someone knowledgeable about Mormons is, "Are they Christian? Do they believe in Christ?" The answer is so unambiguously yes—the name of the religion is after all The Church of Jesus Christ of Latter-day Saints—that it is the question, not the answer, that merits attention. Mormons, like all minorities, live under a stereotype which is both imposed on them and, like all stereotypes, effective because it is believed in by those on whom it is placed. Mormons question themselves because they have begun to believe they are what others say about them. Mormons recognize that they are widely regarded as non-Christian and they attempt to correct that misimpression, to destroy that part of the stereotype which limits some of their freedom, by prominently displaying large pictures or statues of Christ in the temple precincts.

Mormons also know they are easily labelled peculiar and even un-American. As with the Salt Lake Temple and many others, the main approach has a huge American flag flying in front of the towers of the temple. These towers were once the visible symbol of all that was loudly anti-American within Mormonism, and the viewer can now see them only within the context of the national flag. This display is meant to tell the viewer that this church is loyal to America, and hints at the depths of its American character.

Using rather obvious devices like the stereotyped portrayals of Christ, American flags and the purest American building styles, Mormons attack two of the most common mistakes used to isolate them as a minority group. The temple proclaims them to be both Christian and American and attempts to change the stereotype.

With data of this sort we begin to see that we are not looking at just a religious building, we are looking at a political one as well. And once we see that, a whole volume of material comes into play. Mormons regard their church "as true," that is founded by Christ using his Prophet Joseph Smith, Jr.; they believe the Second Coming will take place in America, and more precisely in Independence, Missouri, which was also the scene of the Garden of Eden; they hold the United States Constitution to be divinely inspired, and if it is not a revealed document like the Bible, it is the next thing to it. They feel the Second Coming is imminent and that it will be preceded by the decay and fall of earthly governments—including our own. We need not dwell on the accuracy of that prediction, just on the potential use a millennial religion can make of it. Mormons feel that in the days just before the destruction of the world and the Second Coming, they, and more accurately their priesthood—whose orders are represented in the six towers on the temple—will save the Constitution by holding the reigns of government after massive evil has corrupted the normal run of office-holders. Seen in this light the temple now becomes not just a political statement, it has become the active launching site for political millennialism. This is part of the political ideology expressed in theological terms that is represented in this temple. It is what can be read out of the building, and knowing Mormon ideology, what can be read into the building.

The Washington Temple is a political move designed to challenge and change national conceptions about Mormons. It is also a device for making Mormonism into a national religion. When seen as such we can also see why it is such an unusual national church, and such an unusual Mormon temple. In being the biggest and most expensive, as well as the most prominent temple Mormons have ever built, they announce their shift to the east, out of the western desert. The temple announces Mormon political ambitions both to the non-Mormon world and to themselves. In this sense the Mormons have built neither a challenge to national churches, nor just another Mormon temple; they have built a challenge to the national capital. And insofar as we see this ideological artifact as a political building in theological guise, we can begin to fathom its deeper purpose. The temple is a very real and quite concrete challenge to the present conception of things in the United States, as the Mormons think they perceive them.

It is one thing to announce a challenge to a dominant worldview, and quite another to bring it about. But by building a carefully conceived and executed monument to hasten desired political changes the Mormons are acting in a very old and successful tradition. Every utopian group, including Mormons in the nineteenth century, set out to modify behavior by modifying the physical environment the believers lived in (Kanter 1972:74–126; Leone 1972: 125–150). The construction of a physical setting whose form was both to enable and enforce desired behavior and attitudes is behind the sacred technology found in almost every American utopia, and indeed in almost every utopia in the western world. That this nineteenth century tradition, which was a conscious part of Mormonism, should be expressed in its most recent temple comes, then, as no surprise.

However, more than a utopian tradition of behavior modification through technological determinism is involved here. Anyone who has ever walked through St. Peter's in the Vatican understands the principle that the prestige that a religious hierarchy wants to achieve can be brought about by building a monument to itself. St. Peter's was begun with the return of the papacy to Rome after the Babylonian Captivity in Avignon. It was a low point in the papacy's power and prestige and coincided with the announcement of plans to rebuild St. Peter's. The plan of course, even though not fully completed for two centuries, celebrated the central position, the authenticity, and the glory of the papacy. It did this, as the old basilica built by Constantine did not; but it did build, like its predecessor over one of the chief pilgrimage spots in Christendom. The popes combined massive pilgrim traffic with architectural statements about their own importance to achieve a level of prestige they had never before enjoyed.

As a political act the Mormon temple has two constituencies: Mormons and non-Mormons. Its effect on Mormons is more precise and calculated. The temple serves the many tens of thousands of Saints in the eastern United States, eastern Canada, and the Caribbean. Since a Mormon ought to go through the temple once a year or more, the Washington Temple will refocus the pilgrimage traffic of up to a third of a million Mormons with all the economic, political, and emotional shifts that entails. I would have guessed that such refocussing would have sponsored both a looser integration of eastern Saints into the church in general, and more independence for this traditionally more liberal group of Mormons. But all Mormons I spoke to stressed that the Washington Temple would bind them more closely to the church and make them feel as though they were on a more equal footing with those in Utah. What seems to be behind the feeling of greater equality, and behind having a temple as well, is the notion of gift-giving as a way of creating subordination and undermining independence. Eastern Mormons have long been troublesome to the church, which was happy to have growth in the East but was unused to the degree of liberalism and sophistication that that particular growth brought into the church. To this population which often felt distant and less than well-integrated into the church, the institution then announced that it would pay eleven of the re-

quired fifteen million dollars for the new temple. This gift was met with a response from eastern Mormons who raised six million as opposed to the four Salt Lake stipulated. This has two meanings it seems to me. The first is spontaneous gratitude at being included in the ranks of normal (having a temple readily available) Mormons. Second, the response gives part of Salt Lake's gift back. Gifts require reciprocity by creating a debt. In giving part of the gift back eastern Mormons indicated that the Church underestimated their strength and loyalty, and indicated too that closer integration into the church meant a loss of certain unspecified independence which is gone once the gift is accepted. So from both sides the temple as a gift will create a tighter Mormon community: more closely integrated in the East because they raised so much money, and more closely tied to church headquarters in the West, since the temple was an overwhelming gift and must be acknowledged as such.

The temple will aid church growth and visibility in the outside world. The name of everyone who visited the temple was taken down along with an address. Mormons plan to have missionaries call on that ocean of 800,000 visitors in the year and a half after dedication. Here they are employing a self-selected population to enhance the likelihood of their own growth. Since a large percentage of all Mormons in the Northeast are converts made at the Mormon pavillion at the last New York World's Fair, the Washington Temple represents the same missionizing model on a larger and more permanent scale.

Four million of the fifteen million dollars the temple cost was to be raised in the Mormon areas the temple was being built to serve. In effect, this meant the Mormons in east coast cities. This may amount to 40,000 Mormons spread between Washington, New York, and Boston. This relatively small group raised at least 50% more than they were called on to raise. General tithing funds from the church paid for the rest of the building, this being the usual policy whenever any temple or ward chapel is built. This fact says more than that the east coast Mormons are successful people who make heavy donations or heavy sacrifices to their church.

The capacity to raise vast amounts of money among a group of people who are scattered and provincial in relation to the source of power bears some attention. By making many hitherto autonomous entities dependent on an organizing hierarchy, a new level of efficiency is created. It is a mistake to take a giant building effort as an index of political coherence; it is the means to guarantee that power and centralization will follow as was the case with St. Peters. Keynes called this deficit spending, but its real purpose is the economic success that follows from the organization required by a massive construction effort (Mendelssohn 1971: 210–220). A labor like the Washington Temple brings cooperative effort and efficiency in fund-raising to a new peak for Mormons in the East. The successful execution of such a labor equips the area's Mormons with organizational machinery of a scope and kind different from what existed before the building of the temple, and one capable of drawing more converts and of placing those converts in better jobs as a result of more people knowing Mormon behavioral traits, and of more Mormons to do the hiring. With more and better jobs, Mormons feel their religion is worthy and true and credit the building of their community and specifically of its temple to Divine Providence. All this illustrates how building the Washington Temple affected hundreds of thousands of people.

After showing that the building and operation of the new temple actually have concrete, real effect on the non-Mormon and Mormon population and after realizing that this rather static building is in fact quite active in terms of what its advent and use have organized, it is important to return to the temple's more peculiar characteristics: its isolation. It is closed, it is not in downtown Washington with the other national religious buildings, its architecture is peculiar. It is a massively confusing paradox: it is not identified, its use is secret, it is a closed magnet in the sense that it draws but does not draw inside; it tempts but does not satisfy. It looks very American, but represents a theocracy; it flies the flag but access is not democratic. The building like the religion and the people it repre-

sents is American and Mormon, similar but not the same, living in the same place and members of the same culture but not unified; very close but ultimately, by Mormon desire and American compliance, exclusive. So the basic structure repeats itself, and does so while playing on some similar inclinations in American culture itself.

> But the placing of the temple near Washington, but not in it, suggests . . . impulses to be near but not in the main culture. The idea of the temple as closed to the public [suggests] they are using the American drive for discovery, success, achievement, ladder-climbing as a lure for getting people into the church in every sense of that word. Here is a secret every American can not have—a club he must join before entering—Such a message would have special appeal for the wealthy, success-motivated easterners. Even the theology which projects three levels of heaven is attuned to the mentality of status and ladder-climbing. Along the same lines, the idea of a secret has long had great appeal for Americans who live in a society which is supposedly open and democratic. Here is a group which admits that there is a secret to be kept—is the secret in a way its bigotry? Does the church have special appeal to white middle class people who are at heart racist but want religious conversion and theology to justify their racism? Such conservative Americans always know . . . that the Federal government is eventually going to cause them to give up yet another true American ideal as the country moves from tradition to Communism (Elliott 1975).

The temple takes advantage of a tension-ridden situation to communicate its message. It provides a quite peaceful and wholly enveloping scheme for the non-Mormon visitor just off the Beltway. In taking the tour of the visitor's center and grounds, which anyone is welcome to, one is confronted with the promises Mormonism holds out, as well as the withholding of a glimpse of what ultimate peace and coherence look like inside the temple. The American can get close but not across. He is confronted with the basic structure of the Mormon worldview: you can not be American and Mormon, the two must remain distinct in order for the latter to continue to exist. The two categories must exist but not cross or mix. Only in this way can the Mormon, in his own eyes, help show America the way. And only in this way can America continue to make use of the Mormon minority. The casual tourist is the potential convert, but he has to have been at odds with his own system before the paradoxes highlighted by the Mormon temple strike him and allow him to appreciate the resolutions Mormonism has waiting for him inside. The temple basically, is about joy. Mormons say this. But joy cannot be experienced without the preceding pain; Mormons do not say that, but instead have located the temple in such a way as to bring the receptive visitor into maximum confrontation with how unsatisfying the world is as he is currently experiencing it.

The Mormon too, like everybody else, experiences pain in the form of the problems of everyday life. But in helping him to resolve the pain, which is what the temple experience is for, it helps the believer come to terms with the profundity of it. In making it more conscious and in sharing it with others the temple rites give it meaning, organize it and consequently assuage it. But because of the structure of Mormonism, the pain can neither be resolved nor finally eliminated. The structure insists on separation and can only relax the resultant tension. And the tension must remain because of the structure of Mormonism.

It is appropriate to ask what brought such a structure into existence and what makes it continue. I think the answer to these two questions will show why the paradox of its structure can not be resolved. The historical origins of close but non-overlapping categories lies in Mormonism's nineteenth century utopian history, a history made up of a long struggle, so characteristic of American utopias, between removal and alienation from the parent society on the one hand, and a plan, on the other, to show that same parent a way to a better and more perfect version of itself. Mormons were in rebellion, but did not intend to be independent. In trying cooperative ventures, novel family relations, direct revelation to a prophet and a theocratic government, Mormons attempted to solve many of the social ills common to the early industrial United States and western Europe. These experiments brought them persecution for their pains and forced Mormons from New York, Ohio, Missouri, and Illinois. They went finally to the completely empty (of whites) Great

Basin and Utah. Driven ever farther from America with every effort to improve life within it, they did not want to be anything less than American citizens. For Mormons the U.S. Constitution remained a divinely inspired document and the Utah Mormons tried to obtain statehood many times before success was reached in 1896. All this and far more information supports the basic historical tension arising from wanting to perfect America, wanting to be separate from it, being persecuted by it, and never being independent of it. Throughout the nineteenth century Mormons were inside and outside American society at the same time: in rebellion, but to be a vanguard. From 1847 when they entered Utah, to 1896 and statehood, the Mormon population was to some degree really isolated from the rest of the United States. For the early part of that period the Mormons were all but politically independent, which meant that the pull between being Mormon and being American was not so strong, and meant, further, that in isolation the differences that came to characterize Mormonism could and even had to be well-developed.

With the federal government's active campaign against plural marriage in the 1880s and 1890s, with statehood, and with the economic development of the area by non-Mormon railroads, mines, timber and agricultural interests came two forces to change—or perhaps better—to highlight the nature of Mormonism's relationship to the country as a whole. A large and vocal anti-Mormon population entered the state, and second, eastern capital possessed its economy at the same time that federal agencies replaced the church's economic institutions which had previously underwritten the area's economic self-sufficiency. Thus, by 1900, Utah was reduced from economic self-sufficiency to colonial dependency. While earlier it was possible to be Mormon and American because the worst aspects of the latter did not enter isolated Utah, now with the beginning of the twentieth century, it was necessary to come to terms with living in both Mormondom and America and doing so closely and simultaneously.

Mormons began to live in an economic setting where they were in competition with other Anglos, Chicanos, and several American Indian groups. Moreover they had lost control over their economy. This set of circumstances produced a population maximally responsive to external change and which has become, as a result, highly successful at exploiting its own colonized situation. "Mormons make the best second-in-commanders in the world" epitomizes the Mormon worldview that has evolved in the course of the twentieth century. I have detailed elsewhere (1974) how the process of adjusting to rapid change and rationalizing flexibility works. But here it is surely enough to say that what we see these people living in is a world of high ambiguity, incoherence and arbitrariness. They live in it in such a way that they exploit these very features of it and build success by utilizing them. Mormons can do this by keeping the world divided into categories—but special categories—whose contradictions they do not attempt to resolve, but rather accept. This means that they rarely have to bother with synthesizing myriad contradictions, but rather, juggle at will.

Fascinating as this sounds, I think it is also accurate, and can happen only in the face of nearly total blindness to what is happening. Probably the most noticeable feature of a Mormon when you meet him is his certainty. He not only "knows" his church to be true and Joseph to have been a prophet of God, he is certain he understands what life is about, his place in it and his role in the past and future. He has the answers—and he really does. Producing that certainty are experiences and institutions like the temple which takes the categories a Mormon lives with, calls them true, necessary and painful; shows the bliss that comes from being valiant in the face of them; takes the fear out of them by immersing him in them inside the temple; and then sends the individual back out to start again.

ACKNOWLEDGEMENTS

I am particularly indebted to Professors Jean-Paul Dumont, Emory Elliott and James Boon for long conversations on the substance and theory in this paper. Professor John Gager clarified points in his own work for me. Professors Charles Peterson and John Sorenson read drafts of this paper and made valuable comments on it. I am indebted to George S. Tanner and Robert L. Schuyler for their help in assessing the sensitivity of some of the material in this paper. Alfred Bush made very important corrections on the place of the individual in the temple rites. A helpful conversation with Lewis Binford at the time this paper was read allowed me to keep in mind how much the work here departs from positivist epistemology.

David and Janice Allred and David Tolman patiently answered my questions about the temple and taught me its importance for Mormons. I am grateful to them.

The firsthand impressions of the Washington Temple were gathered during a tour in September 1974 while the building was open to the public.

Permission has been granted by *The New Yorker* for the quote by Calvin Trillin.

Department of Anthropology
University of Maryland

Bibliography

DEETZ, JAMES F.
1974 A cognitive historical model for American material culture, 1620–1835. In Reconstructing complex societies, edited by Charlotte B. Moore. Supplement to the *Bulletin of the Schools of American Research*, No. 20.

DOLGIN, JANET
1974 Latter-day sense and substance. In *Religious movements in contemporary America*, edited by I. I. Zaretsky and M. P. Leone. Princeton University Press, Princeton.

ELLIOTT, EMORY
1975 Personal letter of June 17.

GAGER, JOHN G.
1975 *Kingdom and community, the social world of early Christianity*. Prentice Hall, Inc., Englewood Cliffs.

KANTER, ROSABETH M.
1972 *Commitment and community, communes and utopias in sociological perspective*. Harvard University Press, Cambridge.

LEONE, MARK P.
1972 Archaeology as the science of technology: Mormon townplans and fences. In *Research and theory in current archaeology*, edited by C. L. Redman. Wiley-Interscience, John Wiley and Sons, New York.
1974 The economic basis for the evolution of Mormon religion. In *Religious movements in contemporary America*, edited by I. I. Zaretsky and M. P. Leone. Princeton University Press, Princeton.

LÉVI-STRAUSS, CLAUDE
1963 The effectiveness of symbols. In *Structural anthropology*. Basic Books, New York.

MCCONKIE, BRUCE R.
1966 *Mormon doctrine*. Bookcraft, Salt Lake City.

MENDELSSOHN, KURT
1971 A scientist looks at the pyramids. *American Scientist* 59:210–220.

PANOFSKY, ERWIN
1955 *Meaning in the visual arts*. Doubleday and Company, Inc., Garden City.

ROWE, JOHN H.
1965 The renaissance foundations of anthropology. *American Anthropologist* 67:1–20.

TRILLIN, CALVIN
1970 March 20, U. S. journal: Provo, Utah, categories. In *The New Yorker*, New York.

WHALEN, WILLIAM J.
1964 *The Latter-day Saints in the modern day world*. University of Notre Dame Press, Notre Dame.

The Structure of
Historical Archaeology
and the Importance
of Material Things

James E. Fitting

THE TASK OF A DISCUSSANT at a symposium is fairly clear. He is to listen carefully to the papers and hear what they have to say in themselves and what they have to say as a group. He is to point out the strengths and weaknesses of individual presentations and deal with their complementary nature. In relating divergent styles and paradigms, he is to be, in Leland Ferguson's words of instruction, "pragmatic and cogent."

A symposium is a living thing with a group of real people sitting on a single platform. They are constantly reacting to each other and to an audience. Facial expressions, body language, audience feedback and the style of the script which each participant uses to take notes on the presentations of the other participants are a part of the "happening." At Charleston, South Carolina, the symposium on "Historical Ar-

chaeology and the Importance of Material Things" started as a morning session. The ideas discussed at the session infiltrated many of the other sessions. A hall was provided for an additional four hours of evening discussion and this ran on in informal talks for entire nights in hotel rooms, bars and restaurants. I have a large file of correspondence including the cross checking of references and review from after the meeting. At the Philadelphia meeting in 1976, a few diehards continued the dialog.

Well over a year after the original meeting, I received copies of the revised papers from the symposium; some substantially altered and enlarged, others essentially the same as they were presented. I had 1) the preliminary copies of the symposium papers, 2) my notes and observations on these papers, 3) my notes on the papers as they were presented, 4) a tape of the synthesis of the two sets of notes and 5) the revised set of papers prepared after the symposium. Was the discussant to become the book reviewer? Or was it still possible to capture some of the exuberance of the actual symposium? I have chosen the latter course with the hope that some of what occurred in Charleston can transcend the studied limitations of the printed word. Glassie really did talk about his conversations with Irish peasants around peat fires and Binford did respond with an acid and predictable preface to his written paper in response to Deetz's presentation. These occurrences, and many others, were portions of the symposium excluded from the present volume.

While the focus of the symposium was on material things, the analytical mode was structural. It was delightful to participate in an archaeological symposium where Lévi-Strauss was one of the most cited sources. My analysis of the symposium was also structural. Ferguson presented his concepts of the structure of the symposium in preliminary correspondence. Added to this is my structural analysis of Ferguson's structure and the final structures of the symposium and the papers which have come from the symposium. There are enough levels of "reality" with all the inherent transformations, to confuse even Lévi-Strauss.

An essential part of any structure is symmetry, or the available transformations to account for symmetry, or Bororo villages of archaeology. Several key elements were included in the initial planning for the symposium which are not in this volume. David Clarke was scheduled to participate but was unable to attend. Robert Ascher was invited to participate but was unable to do so. Both Clarke and Ascher represent essential positions for the study of the structure of the study of material things and *Analytical Archaeology* and "Tin*Can Archaeology," recently published in *Historical Archaeology*, are real and vivid parts of the symposium which are not included in this volume. These are part of the "missing data" which is included in this analysis.

There are a number of a priori assumptions used in these papers, even by those who would theoretically deny the existence of a priori assumptions. The first of these, and here I paraphrase the logical positivist Ernst Mach, deals with the knowability of material things. The world does not consist of mysterious things; but things, in themselves, in association with an ego, produce sensations; sensations, as directly observed, are realities. This leads to the tacit exclusions of several systems of thought; systems which define observations as being dependent on the observer are excluded although this excludes several basic rationalistic systems of thought that are very close to structuralism. Mystical systems are also excluded and neither Khalil Gibran or Carlos Casteneda are included on the program. Leone's paper, however, suggests that nonrationalistic belief systems can have an effect on material things and that mystical systems should not be dismissed out of hand. Perhaps there is something worthwhile beyond our *tonal*.

Therefore, we are left with material things as a starting point; that is, with the idea that a material thing can be studied. In reality, the attributes which a material thing may possess are infinite. It would be safe to state that at no time has anyone done a complete descriptive study, let alone an analytical study, of a single material object. Such a study would be physically and psychologically impossible. We all utilize a series of preselected attributes, and the conclusions drawn from such a study are circumscribed by our philosophical framework; by the operative paradigms of the analyst including his criterion of "proof."

The analogy of the blind man and the elephant used by Deetz is particularly appropriate. We are all blind men looking at elephants and our interpretations of elephants are as diverse as the parts of the elephant that we are allowed to touch. The parts which we are allowed to touch are artifacts of our theoretical orientation. A corollary of this is that our blindness is, in effect, our vision.

A further limitation to this symposium is an accident of participation and might have been avoided if Ascher were here. Jean Piaget, in *A Structural Study of the Sciences of Man*, has divided the sciences of man into, (1) nomothetic and (2) historical and, of lesser interest to us, (3) legal sciences and (4) philosophical disciplines. Nomothetic sciences seek to identify "laws," or regularities in human behavior. They operate in what Lévi-Strauss has called "statistical" time which is noncumulative and reversible. They generate models which some archaeologists might call processual. Historical sciences are those which propose to reconstruct or reconstitute events as they have happened in the past. These are idiosyncratic analyses. The object is mechanical models, using Lévi-Strauss' term, which duplicate the event and exist within a time frame which is irreversible and continuous. This distinction between mechanical and statistical models and time, between nomothetic and historical paradigms, is one of the major sources of failure to communicate in contemporary archaeology.

In spite of the nomothetic nature of the symposium papers, it is possible that the majority of the membership of the Society for Historical Archaeology think in terms of mechanical time and have the reconstruction of actual events as a goal. With their tacit acceptance of statistical time, most of these papers may be misdirected. As an aside, Piaget sees the maturation of historical sciences in the process of history becoming part of disciplines rather than existing as a field in itself. Therefore, the Society for Historical Archaeology may be a part of a predictable process as the nomothetic approaches of archaeology incorporate the idiosyncratic data of history into, as Iain Walker has proposed, a single discipline.

Given this basic background to the symposium, it is possible to approach each of the individual presentations. Ferguson has set that stage for the symposium by calling, first, for an extension of our vision, for a new emphasis on material things that is perhaps carried to its conclusion in Deetz's paper suggesting that universities develop Departments of Material Things. Another important observation is that both the historical and archaeological records can be studied as real entities in themselves. This may produce divergent conclusions but this is a result of the peculiar blindnesses of each. They may be contradictory but both

can be logically, even "scientifically" studied.

I would tend to disagree with his observations on the convergence of attitudes. I do not believe that it exists or can exist; and this is based, in part, on an interchange of letters with Iain Walker several years ago. This interchange did not result in a convergence but rather in an agreement to disagree. More important than convergence is the recognition of diversity. An *interdisciplinary* study, developing a single paradigm, is very different from the *multidisciplinary* study, with a series of mutually coexisting paradigms, which seems to be developing in historical archaeology. Ferguson may be correct but tolerance may be a better word for what has been happening than convergence.

Deetz made several key points of which the most important might have been the importance of not taking anything in archaeology too seriously. On one level, this might mean that we become ridiculous when we lose our ability to laugh at ourselves. On another level, it points to the transient nature of "truth." Glassie has his folklorist spying on anthropologists, who are spying on linguists, who are spying on physicists. In an age where such immutable "facts" as the speed of light and elemental particles are changing everyday, we might all be better off reading Blake. All archaeological "conclusions" will certainly be revised and the difference between a "bad" and a "good" archaeological report may be in the number of months that is required to alter its conclusions. It is courting ridicule, if not disaster, to stand by "old" interpretations in the face of new data. As a result, the individual who is taken the least seriously by others is the one who takes himself most seriously.

As I followed Deetz's presentation, I took a series of notes. "Is Deetz a silent structuralist?" "Is this Sassurian Archaeology?" And finally, "Anyone who quotes *Tristes Tropiques* can't be all bad." Deetz has made an elegant case for the importance of structural analysis in archaeology, far more eloquently and subtly than any that has gone before and to realize this requires more than his symposium paper, although *Invitation to Archaeology* is a good starter.

I have often wondered why structuralism,

with its obvious applications to the study of material things, has either been ignored or rejected by American archaeologists. While essentially positivistic, it has developed from the intellectual traditions of rationalism rather than Anglo-American empiricism, although it claims to be empirical. The divergence is in the definitions of reality and the criteria of proof. As Bob Scholte phrased it in an article in *American Anthropologist* in 1966, "The protagonists of the French anthropological tradition generally assume the primacy of the human mind, their investigations proceed along formal and structural lines, and their questions are posed in synchronic-relational and deductive terms. The adherents of the Anglo-American tradition, in its widest sense, assume the primacy of the behavioral act, their methods are essentially quantitative and descriptive, and their problems are phrased in diachronic-causal and empirically inductive terms."

The preacher in Ecclesiastes had the answer, "There is nothing new under the sun." The arguments used by the students of both Descartes and Spinoza against the empiricism of Bacon are, in essence, the only refutations needed to defend rationalism against empiricism. Empiricism is an essential element of positivism but so is rationalism. So structuralism and positivistic archaeology converge, at least in the structural interpretation, in spite of the protestations of both. They are at opposite poles only within a very limited universe.

Still, Binford's paper following that presented by Deetz, was a major contrast; much more of a contrast than that of subject matter. Binford's symposium reactions to Deetz's paper were even more predictable.

Binford represents the position of logical positivism. His conscious, or unconscious antecedents, as Robert Butler pointed out in his review of *An Archaeological Perspective*, can be traced to the "Vienna School" of the early 20th century. It is significant that the more prominent members of this school, such as Moritz Schlick, came from the "hard" sciences rather than philosophy. The stated goal of the school was the exclusion of metaphysics and the concentration on empirically verifiable realities.

Binford has emphasized this point and criticized "intuitional" interpretations as being nonverifiable metaphysics (and poorly reasoned metaphysics at that). The interesting result has been that he has opened the door to a wider range of potential interpretations by forcing the workaday archaeologists to ask themselves "Exactly what is verifiable?"

At this point, we need to insert one of the missing elements of the symposium, the paper that should have been presented by David Clarke. Binford and Clarke need to be considered at one time because, in spite of the disclaimers of both, they are considered as similar by so many others.

Binford's analysis of how he differs from Clarke sounds, to the Aristotelian, like St. Augustine's argument with the Platonists; Tweedle Dee and Tweedle Dum. Like St. Augustine and the Platonists, there is a real difference. Clarke's intellectual tradition goes back through Hume and Locke to Bacon. It is eminently logical and leads to the formulation of constructs from material things that must be accepted as real even though they are untestable. As Ferguson quoted earlier, "archaeology is archaeology is archaeology."

This brings us into the realm of what Piaget has called "metasociological" interpretation or back to the metaphysics that the positivists initially rejected. The term which we might use would be "meta-archaeological." Although this has a most unpopular sound, it might not be all that bad. Albert Einstein and Max Planck were, in the truest sense of the word, metaphysical in many of their formulations. They could not be directly proven and could be tested only through axiomatic corollaries. Their concepts form the basis of modern physics. If physicists can be metaphysical, why should archaeologists not be meta-archaeological? Both should read Blake.

The paper which Binford did present had many interesting attributes. It does manage to relate the study of a contemporary Eskimo community to the study of Middle Paleolithic artifacts. What Binford intended to be the main point of his paper, however, is not necessarily what I would consider to be the most outstanding part. I immediately recalled the moment of first contact with the natives, the frustration of conflicting data and the exhilaration at the finding of order that Lévi-Strauss recorded in *Tristes Tropiques*.

Is Binford practicing the positivist's vice of humanism in public? Will this not lead to rationalism? It is not Deetz who is our secret structuralist, but rather Binford. We may have finally uncloaked a fundamentalist M.D. who has misled us into believing that he is a Unitarian chiropractor. And this leads us back to Deetz's observation that we should not take any of this too seriously.

Glassie's paper gives us, as archaeologists, a chance to see ourselves as others see us. It also gives added weight to Deetz's observation that material things are not the sole property of the archaeologist and that the Department of Material Things needs to be open to many people currently housed in other academic Balkan countries. I think that this comes out in Leone's paper as well.

Glassie's candid observations on the search for novel paradigms in folklore are certainly familiar. I am sure that many of his colleagues are as certain that they are dealing with certain truth as are the archaeologists with "science" flowing in their veins. When "truth" is served out by the zealot, the quest for truth itself is lost. So we borrow, and discover Blake anew through the physicists, and go back to the drawing board for a new look at our old, old problems.

Glassie comes back to Lévi-Strauss as the creator of a completely open system of thought. There are other open systems as well but this one is rigorous enough to convince the humanist that he is being scientific long enough that he no longer cares about it. Lévi-Strauss was an avowed positivist when he wrote *Elementary Structures of Kinship*, but noted in his second preface to the English translation that he no longer understood it and failed to see why it had excited so many people. In the final volume of the *Mythologiques*, he questions the existence of a "science" of man. As I suggested in a book review in *Science* in 1972, is the objective study of subjectivity more objective than the subjective study of subjectivity?

There is another point that is well taken in this paper. A rigorous intellectual approach works very well for the solution of very small problems. It has less application to the solution of bigger problems like the existence of God and the place of man in the Universe. How can the positivist generate an hypothesis on the nature of beauty, not the beauty of a specific culture but as a universal concept? It may be easy to win a game at a very small chessboard but who is to say that the actual squares do not extend to the ends of the Universe?

The Tuscon Garbage Project is something apart from the other papers. It is more in the line of a traditional site report on a larger scale. Its conclusions are essentially inductive and, although it has been supported and praised by "useful" organizations, its ultimate contribution is still inchoate. In some respects, it is nomothetic and positivistic in its goals. It sounds somewhat like the voluntaristic positivism of Parsonian Sociology.

Leone's paper is difficult to deal with since, in many respects, he goes beyond the symposium to deal with some of the major problems in western culture. One thing that was immediately striking about this paper was the objective and scientific description of the temple and its function. This seemed to parallel Michael Valentine Smith's temple in Robert Heinlein's *Stranger in a Strange Land* in an uncanny fashion.

The paper has also dealt with material things not necessarily as the product of a culture but as the determinant of it. This is the "houses make people" approach and it places Leone in a category with Palao Solari and Buckminster Fuller. The logical conclusions of this line of thought lead back to the eventual limits of knowability. This recognition of the limits of knowledge within any single logical system has been hinted at in several of these papers and finds a fuller expression in William Irwin Thompson's *At the Edge of History*. As with several papers in this symposium, Thompson comes back to the importance of introspection, reflective thought and the basic, rather than scientific, problems of mankind.

There is another door which Leone has opened for us. In the *New York Times* review of Zaretsky and Leone's *Religious Movements in*

Contemporary America, the book was applauded for its recognition that religious systems could be studied as entities having validity in themselves rather than simply as objects viewed through the lenses of other ideological systems. Leone has invited us to see the internal structure, and validity, of mystical systems and if we follow through, we might have Carlos Casteneda's observations on the importance of material things, the *tonal*, at a future meeting.

Mention should be made at this point of some of the missing data, particularly Robert Ascher's "Tin＊Can Archaeology." While empirically based, it is essentially idealistic rather than positivistic. There might be some question as to the use of "empirical idealism" as a logical category. As I recall, it has been used before, and even presented in an algebraic formula in the famous Footnote B in Talcott Parson's *Structure of Social Action*. It certainly helps to round out the structure of the symposium.

In the few weeks prior to the symposium, I became aware of still another philosophical tradition which might have been incorporated as well. This is Hans Vaihinger's philosophy of *als-ob*, or as-if. It has also been referred to as "fictionalism." Vaihinger's fictionalism is of an extreme sort and he maintains that fictional constructs of the mind "contradict" reality and, in the case of the boldest and most successful, are self-contradictory. He makes a distinction between hypotheses, which are real, and fictions, which are hypotheses which have been accepted as true. The result is a logical system where you are absolutely certain that you are wrong as soon as you accept anything as absolutely certain. It is interesting that historians of philosophy, notably Ledger Wood, have classified this as "idealistic positivism" which would place it well within the symmetrical structure of this symposium.

Systems of thought are, or should be, internally consistent. They are defined by what they are, not what they are not. Idealism is not the antithesis of positivism and rationalism is not the antithesis of humanism. Furthermore, all systems have their own historical development and none is really closed, for all do continue to develop and change. Our "elephant" of material things has been viewed in many different ways. The presentations in this volume, and related approaches within the structure, have included, both empirical and humanistic rationalism, logical and voluntaristic positivism, empirical idealism and idealistic positivism. In addition to material things, structuralism has also been a persistent elephant in both recognized and unrecognized forms.

The results of the symposium have been varied. We have seen what can be done with material things using different conceptual tools. The most important result of the symposium, as I see it, is the recognition and definition of our conceptual heterogeneity, the recognition of paradigmatic pluralism. The past debates to which Ferguson referred now appear to be sterile name calling; a false opposition in a varied world. Our future is not in unified theory, the selection of a single blindness, but in the realization that "truths" arrived at with different criterion of proof, are as true as those of our own, even if they contradict each other. We should hope for a greater understanding of "method" rather than violent reactions to transient "conclusions."

There is also a word of warning here as well. The blindnesses, or conceptual frameworks, which we select for the study of material things are no more than a part of the tools which we use in this study; the intellectual trowels, backhoes and calipers of the archaeologists. There is the persistent danger that these tools may become more important than the objects of study themselves. It is at this point that we will have reached, as Ferguson and Deetz have warned us, the point of "sterile methodological virtuosity."

Gilbert/Commonwealth
Jackson, Michigan

Bibliography

ASCHER, ROBERT
 1975 Tin*Can archaeology. *Historical Archaeology* VIII: 7–16.

BUTLER, ROBERT
 1974 Review of *An archaeological perspective*, by Lewis R. Binford. *American Antiquity* 39(4), pt. 1:646–647.

CLARKE, DAVID
 1968 *Analytical archaeology*. Methuen & Co., London.

COX, HARVEY
 1974 Review of *Religious movements in contemporary America*, edited by I. I. Zaretsky and Mark P. Leone. *New York Times Review of Books*, Dec. 22, 1974, p. 13.

DEETZ, JAMES
 1967 *Invitation to archaeology*. Natural History Press, New York.

FITTING, JAMES
 1972 Book review: archeology and science. *Science* 175(4025):976–977.

HEINLEIN, ROBERT A.
 1961 *Stranger in a strange land*. Putnam, New York.

LÉVI-STRAUSS, CLAUDE
 1969 *The elementary structure of kinship*. Beacon Press, Boston.
 1973 *Tristes tropiques*. Jonathon Cape, London.

PARSONS, TALCOTT
 1949 *The structure of social action; a study in social theory with special reference to a group of recent European writers*. Free Press, Glencoe, Illinois.

PIAGET, JEAN
 1970 *A structural study of the sciences of man*. Harper Torchbooks, New York.

SCHOLTE, BOB
 1966 Epistemic paradigms: some problems in cross-cultural research on social anthropological history and theory. *American Anthropologist* 68(5): 1192–1201.

THOMPSON, WILLIAM I.
 1971 *At the edge of history*. Harper-Colophon, New York.

WALKER, IAIN
 1967 Historic archaeology—methods and principles. *Historical Archaeology* 1967 I: 23–34.

Afterword: "To Make Us Good People," A Reflection on the 1975 Thematic Symposium of the Annual Meeting of the Society for Historical Archaeology, Charleston, South Carolina

Leland Ferguson

Although he later had second thoughts, this volume began with Stanley South. In the early 1970s, South was arguably the best-known historical archaeologist in the country. Other contenders included Ivor Noel Hume, James Deetz, and Charles Fairbanks. Together with South these men held the ground at four of America's historic colonial sites—Plimoth Plantation, Massachusetts (Deetz); Williamsburg, Virginia (Noel Hume); Charles Towne, South Carolina (South); and St. Augustine, Florida (Fairbanks). Of these South had gained notice as founder, in 1960, of the Conference on Historic Sites Archaeology and indefatigable editor of the *Conference Papers,* the first regular publication in the field. In January 1975, the annual meeting of the relatively new Society for Historical Archaeology (SHA, founded in 1967) was to be held in South Carolina—Stanley South's turf.

In anticipation of the meeting, the staff of the South Carolina Institute of Archaeology and Anthropology (SCIAA) spent much of 1974 planning and making preparations. We selected historic Charleston as the meeting site, and Institute Director Robert Stephenson encouraged us to plan for an outstanding meeting. Money was available. This was prior to the recession of the late 1970s and early 1980s, and support came from several flush sources. We funded an open bar on Friday evening and a general invitation banquet with carafes of wine on every table (which got slightly out of hand). There was also enough money to completely cover the travel costs of seven panelists for a plenary symposium.

South was program chairman and he had been disappointed by the papers of the first seven annual meetings of the SHA which he complained had "focused on historical-descriptive, particularistic topics, with little concern shown for the idea-sets under which such topics were explored" (South 1977:1). South wanted a meeting highlighting theory and method in historical archaeology, and as a center piece of the program he imagined a thematic symposium aimed at reinforcing his vision of historical archaeology as an explicitly scientific endeavor aimed at exploring cultural evolution through quantitative analysis, and he asked me to organize the session.

I was relatively young and new at SCIAA, and South's request seemed as much an assignment as a request. I well understood South's approach to historical archaeology. Our backgrounds were somewhat similar. We both grew up in northwestern North Carolina and both attended graduate school with archaeologist Joffre Coe at the University of North Carolina, although I was more than half a dozen years later than South and his well-known digging partner Lewis Binford. South and I had worked, at different times, at Town Creek Indian Mound, North Carolina's premier prehistoric site. There, in Coe's odd way, we were both schooled in his rigorously careful fieldwork and logically based methodology. Although primarily a cultural historian, Coe's connections at the University of Michigan led Binford and South to cultural theorist Leslie White and statistical methodologist Albert Spaulding. I was assigned these works as well. White (e.g., 1949) promoted cultural evolution as a paradigm and positivist science as methodology, and Spaulding (e.g., 1960) developed statistical analyses for archaeological data. These kinds of influences resulted in

Binford's processual archaeology—the largest component of what became known in the late 1960s as the "New Archaeology." South called his variation of this phenomenon "archaeological science," and he expected me to organize a session emphasizing this particular approach.

I appreciated scientific methodology, and I understood processual archaeology. But, I did not find the latter satisfying. The processual approach promised interpretations of social organization and ideology as well as technology, but in practice it dwelt on technological response to environment as an independent, determining variable, and seemed best suited to studies of subsistence behavior, cultural ecology, and long-term cultural development. Religion, cultural philosophy, politics, and social practice played no significant role as causal factors; and straightforward historical explorations of topical issues—such as race or gender—were beyond consideration. For me, my assignment posed a dilemma: Should I invite only scholars whose work I saw as similar to South's scientific archaeology, or should I do something else? My solution was compromise. I invited three panelists I saw as processual archaeologists—Lewis Binford, David Clarke, and William Rathje—and three who were doing something different—James Deetz, Mark Leone, and Robert Ascher. James Fitting accepted an invitation to serve as discussant. He was a dark horse, chosen on recommendation of some of my archaeological cohort. It turned out he had a difficult job that he performed very well.

The differences in the two groups of panelists varied. I considered Deetz and Leone as part of the New Archaeology movement, but different from South and Binford. Early in graduate school I had read James Deetz' monograph (1965) linking ceramic variability to changes in economy and social organization among the historic Arikara of the Missouri valley, and this work seemed similar to Binford's. In contrast, Deetz' small book *Invitation to Archaeology* (1967) proffered an interpretation of material things based on sets of mental rules, a kind of cultural grammar. This kind of normative interpretation of artifacts and assemblages was quite different from processual analyses emphasizing variability. Leone was different in another way, and in at least one way his work was similar to South's. I had read Leone's study of Mormon fence plans (1972), and, in spite of having "Archaeology as the Science of Technology" in the title, therein I saw Leone flirting with religious ideology and social organization as causal factors. Also, this interesting paper involved investigation of a large-scale, aboveground feature, unusual in historical archaeology—although South in his studies of towns and fortifications engaged similar expansive views. They both were dealing with the kind of features now commonly treated in landscape archaeology.

Largely, I think, based on the travel money and the fact that I was representing Stanley South, four of the six archaeologists I invited agreed to attend. Unfortunately, both Clarke and Ascher declined. As discussant James Fitting observed, both of these scholars were "key elements… included in the initial planning for the symposium." Of these, I thought Ascher's absence most disappointing. Clarke's work was well published and similar, in a British way, to Binford's. On the other hand, Ascher's publications, although limited, were the most radically different of the proposed panelists. Together with Charles Fairbanks, Ascher had written an unusual piece of historical archaeology; in an effort to interpret the conditions of bondage, they juxtaposed the soul-stirring words of Depression-era writer James Agee with excavated artifacts from a slave cabin on the coast of Georgia. Then, as we were planning the annual meeting, *Historical Archaeology* included an intriguing paper by Ascher entitled "Tin*Can Archaeology." In this, he presented a case for archaeologists having a unique way of "seeing" material things that had value far beyond archaeology. I was curious to see where this approach might lead and issued an invitation. Had Ascher not left archaeology to make anthropological films, his would likely have become an important voice in responding to the narrow vision of processual archaeology.

Rather than have a session that included only archaeologists, I wanted to have someone for the panel from outside our field and began casting about for an historian. Following a rejection by a well-known social historian, I spoke with James Deetz, and he recommended folklorist Henry Glassie with whom he had worked at Plimoth Plantation. Glassie accepted an invitation and rounded out the panel. It turned out that Deetz and Glassie shared common interest in applying a structural paradigm to material studies. In fact, on the telephone Deetz had said something to the effect that Glassie "had it figured out" and all we had to do was "sit and listen." By "it" we discovered Deetz meant the application of cultural grammar to material studies; and, as it progressed, the session converged to a debate between Binford, and Glassie, processualism vs. structuralism—behavior vs. mental construct. Looking larger, Fitting labeled both approaches as positivistic and concluded that "structuralism and [processualism]… are at opposite poles only within a very limited universe." While these opposite poles became the focus of discussion, on its fringes the symposium pointed to historical archaeology's potential engagement of the larger universe. As Alison Wylie (1993:7) observed "even the most sophisticated positivist models of science… could not begin to make sense of a body of disciplinary practice as complex and multifaceted as archaeology; archaeology, specifically historical archaeology, was much more interesting than that."

The session was well attended and the subsequent publication became a common addition to courses on historical archaeology, particularly those dealing with method and theory. I cannot say the effect the symposium and publication had on the following generation of historical archaeologists; I can, however, testify to my reaction and the effect it had on me. The central messages of the archaeologists on the panel were little different than I expected. Deetz, particularly, was the voice I had been reading in his book and articles. However, beyond their principal points, the other archaeologists—Binford, Leone, and Rathje—offered incidental surprises. Binford claimed to study the Nunamiut of Alaska solely to collect information on the archaeological assemblages of arctic hunters to help explain the "variability as observed in Mousterian materials a continent away and separated from the Nunamiut by at least 60,000 years." Yet, with excitement, he spoke of his introduction to famed hunter Simon Paneack, of his trips to remote hunting sites, of the varied interests of his guides in artifact finds, and of his discovery of exaggerations in ethnologist Helge Ingsted's 1954 book, *Nunamiut*. He requested extra time at the meeting to show slides of his Alaska experience. I understood and appreciated Binford's application of the Nunamiut data to the Mousterian, but I was inspired by his personalized historical archaeology of these arctic hunters.

My reaction to the deliveries by Leone and Rathje were a wow and a grin, respectively. At the symposium, Leone's paper did not contain the detailed structural interpretation included in the published version, rather he seemed focused on the stunning speed with which the Church of Jesus Christ of Latter-day Saints financed and built their symbolically charged Washington Temple. Here was ideological and social power on display. Of course such forces were key components of cultural change and development, especially the kind of short-term change often studied by historical archaeologists. Why did we need to be reminded? With subtle irony, in the published version of his paper, Leone gave credit to a "helpful conversation with Lewis Binford" at the 1975 meeting which allowed him to keep in mind how much his work "depart[ed] from positivist epistemology" (1975: 60). By contrast, Rathje remained faithful to positivist methodology, testing hypotheses on collected behavioral data and drawing conclusions, but with novelty. He was studying us—archaeologically. His findings reinforced that our behavior, and by extension the behavior of those in the past, often contrasts sharply with what we say, and even think, we are doing. The mirror of historical archaeology often reflects a surprise.

Although Henry Glassie's paper argued for a structural approach to material studies, for me a short aside comment in his presentation made a great impression. In reflecting on conflicts between science and the humanities in both archaeology and folklore, Glassie asserted "our methods and theories come most naturally from social sciences, but our goals come most naturally from the humanities" (1977:26-27). He followed this with a triplet: "The reason for our science is to make us good humanists. The reason for our humanism is to make us good scientists. The reason for our study is to make us good people." This was new and thought provoking. I had heard and read many reasons for doing historical archaeology, but "to make us good people" was not one of them. I supposed that "humanism" could be replaced by any moral or ethical system, and I figured "us" should include me personally. Intrigued, I left the meeting thinking that the ultimate goals for archaeological research, in fact for any research, should come from consideration of the human condition, not from science that had value but no values. Thus, the careful identification of worthwhile, achievable goals for archaeological research, and the selection of research topics, was as important, perhaps more important, than the theory and methods employed. Inappropriate method and theory applied in a suitable project toward a worthwhile goal may not take us where we want to go; but applying scientific method and theory without a worthwhile goal would take us nowhere, except by chance. Science has no direction.

Eighteen years after the 1975 meeting my friend and mentor Stanley South lamented (South 1993:16; see also Joseph 2010:141) that "Instead of a special publication oriented toward the scientific analysis and interpretation of material things" the symposium resulted in "a popular volume focusing on structural humanism." For me, South's conclusion misses the mark. The session dealt with two differently oriented and competing scientific paradigms, one completely new to historical archaeology. It also contributed to a blurring of the boundaries between archaeology and other disciplines and helped legitimize a variety of approaches in historical archaeology, including reflexivity and the treatment of topical issues. I was, and continue to be, satisfied that the session participants fulfilled South's original desire (1977:1) to explore the "idea-sets" of archaeological investigation. They offered glimpses of material studies that were provocative, wide ranging, and eye opening.

Bibliography

ASCHER, ROBERT
1974   Tin*Can Archaeology. *Historical Archaeology* 8:7-16.

ASCHER, ROBERT AND CHARLES FAIRBANKS
1971   Excavation of a Slave Cabin: Georgia, U.S.A. *Historical Archaeology* 5:3-17.

BINFORD, LEWIS R.
1965   Archaeological systematics and the study of cultural processes. *American Antiquity*, 31(2), 203-210.

CLARKE, DAVID
1968   *Analytical Archaeology*. Methuen & Co., Ltd., London.

DEETZ, JAMES
1965   The Dynamics of Stylistic Change in Arikara Ceramics. *Illinois Studies in Anthropology*, 4. University of Illinois Press, Urbana.

1967   *Invitation to Archaeology*. The Natural History Press, Garden City, New York.

FERGUSON, LELAND (ED.)
1977   *Historical Archaeology and the Importance of Material Things*. Special Publication Series, No. 2. The Society for Historical Archaeology. Columbia, South Carolina.

JOSEPH, J. W.
2010   *An Interview with Stanley A. South.* Historical Archaeology, 44(2): 132-144.

LEONE, MARK P.
1972   Archaeology as the science of technology: Mormon townplans and fences. In *Research and theory in current archaeology*, edited by C. L. Redman. Wiley-Interscience, John Wiley and Sons, New York.

SOUTH, STANLEY
1993   Strange Fruit: *Historical Archaeology*, 1972-1977. Historical Archaeology, 27(1):15-18.

SPAULDING, ALBERT C.
1960   "The dimensions of archaeology". In Gertrude E. Dole and Robert L. Carneiro (eds). *Essays in the science of culture in hon-*

or of Leslie A. White. New York: Crowell. pp. 437–56.

WYLIE, ALISON
   1993 Invented Land/Discovered Pasts: The Westward Expansion of Myth and History. *Historical Archaeology*, 27(4):1-19.